Woodrow
on the Bench

ALSO BY JENNA BLUM

Those Who Save Us
The Stormchasers
The Lost Family

Woodrow on the Bench

Life Lessons
from a Wise Old Dog

Jenna Blum

HARPER

An Imprint of HarperCollins*Publishers*

HarperCollins books may be purchased for educational, business, or sales promotional use. For information, please email the Special Markets Department at SPsales@harpercollins.com.

FIRST EDITION

Image on page 53 courtesy of the author

Designed by Bonni Leon-Berman

Library of Congress Cataloging-in-Publication Data has been applied for.

ISBN 978-0-06-311318-3

21 22 23 24 25   GV   10 9 8 7 6 5 4 3 2 1

For Woodrow.
And for anyone who's ever loved an old dog.

Woodrow
on the Bench

The Bench

The bench is across the street from my apartment, on a greenway called the Commonwealth Mall that runs from Boston's Public Garden down to Fenway. The Mall striates Commonwealth Avenue like the divider in the middle of Park Avenue in New York City, rendering the street double-wide. Except the Mall has more trees, old-growth oaks and cottonwoods shading it in a gracious canopy. And historical statues on every block: Abigail Adams, Alexander Hamilton, and, on our block, patriot of the Revolution John Glover.

Like any city park, the Mall is lined with benches. Nothing special. Weather-beaten wood supported by curlicued black iron. Some of them have plaques next to them, commemorating people who once loved to sit there. To GINGER, MY CHAMPAGNE LADY, FOR ALL THE SUNSETS. FOR FRED, A FRIEND FOR EVERY SEASON.

Our bench, Woodrow's and mine, has no plaque. It has nothing remarkable about it at all. It's just in closest proximity to where I live, opposite my front door. When I first move into my Back Bay brownstone in 2008, I pay no attention to the bench. I don't even notice it. I have no idea that, eleven years later, when my black Lab Woodrow, then four, has reached the extraordinary age of fourteen, that bench will be our daily destination. Twice a day, in fact.

Now, morning and night in all weathers we will head there, and Woodrow, who can go no farther, WHUMPS down in a patch of dirt his body has made in the grass next to the bench, and it will become our oasis. Neighbors will find us there, and friends and strangers, and I will be a sitting duck for conversation. I will try to work on my iPad and find it impossible. Woodrow will draw people to us like a magnet. The bench, his favorite place, will change my life.

Prologue

In October 2004, my boyfriend suggested we take a day trip. We hopped in my Jeep and drove south out of Boston, toward the Cape. It wasn't unusual for us to do this, to explore the playground of New England, and it was the perfect time for it: the air crisp and cool, the sun still bright, the trees just starting to change into their gold and orange and maroon clothes against the bright-blue sky.

What was unusual was that Andy took an exit before the Sagamore Bridge, toward Duxbury. "Where are we going?" I asked.

"You'll see," he said.

He drove along a winding road bordered by old stone walls, fields, and thickets of trees. Across from a cranberry bog, where thousands upon thousands of berries bobbed in navy-blue water, he pulled into a long driveway leading to a small house with a barn behind it. A saltwater farm? There was a deep-green lawn beneath big old trees, and on the grass, encircled by one of those expandable wooden playpens, tumbled seven Labrador retriever puppies. Five yellow, two black.

"Oh!" I said, opening my door to scramble out before the Jeep had even completely stopped.

"I thought we'd just look," Andy said.

Of course, nobody ever just *looks* at a Labrador puppy. We climbed into the playpen circle and let them bounce all over us, licking us with their tiny puppy tongues, huffing their coffee-smelling puppy breath on our faces, chomping us with their tiny needle teeth. They were so young that they still had their gosling fluff instead of actual fur; their tails had candlewick twists on the ends; their bellies were soft and white and roly-poly, reminding me of one of my favorite Little Golden Books from childhood: *The Poky Little Puppy*.

"I want one!" exclaimed my mom, when I texted her grainy photos from my flip phone. "Let's take the brothers."

The brothers were the two black males. By the time we left an hour later, I had put down a deposit on both, one for me, one for my mom. The breeder tattooed the inside of the pups' ears so we could tell the boys apart.

That was how Woodrow, 01, the more alpha of the two brothers, came to me.

I had not intended to get a dog. It wasn't a good time: Andy had only just moved in, our apartment on Beacon Hill was the size of a postage stamp, I was working as an adjunct writing professor, and I was about to launch my first book. Then again, as people sometimes say about get-ting pregnant—or, in my mom's case, quitting smoking—it's never a good time to get a dog. You might as well dive right in. And who could resist those puppies?

Plus, I was predilected. Dogs were in my family's DNA.

A photo of my mom's great-grandmother Genora, in rural Minnesota, shows a lady in stylish furs, hat, and button-up high-heeled boots—with a square-headed black Lab sitting at her feet. On my dad's side, the legendary and stalwart black Lab Guy was the star of all his childhood memories. My first dog predated me: my mom's cocker spaniel Vivo, a gorgeous, honey-colored AKC champion who loved to hide beneath things—my crib, the Christmas tree, my mom's piano—and attack anyone who came near. The day Vivo, blind and deaf, was scheduled to be taken to the vet to be put to sleep, my dad, who had a long-running feud with the dog, reached down to pet him one last time. "Goodbye, old boy," he said tearfully. Vivo snarled and bit his hand. "Well, the hell with you," my dad said. After that, we had Labs.

Our house in the commuter suburb of Montclair, New Jersey, was a kind of Lab farm when I was growing up. At one point we had three full-grown retrievers banging around: Booda, who was dumb but sweet, with such a bad overbite that seen from below his mouth looked like the shark's on the cover of *Jaws*; Buddy, an elegant, intelligent yellow Lab who posed on Oriental rugs, ate Häagen-Dazs ice cream, and led poor dumb Booda astray, coaxing him into leaving the yard and then abandoning him on unfamiliar streets; and Gus, who was 120 pounds of pure untamed muscle and who, when the doorbell rang, would pick up the nearest object—a tennis racket, a hammer, a lamp—and charge the visitor with it.

You might think that after all this I might not want a Lab of my own, but eight weeks after we saw the pups, we returned to the little farm by the cranberry bog, and the Jones boys, as we called them—Woodrow Jones and Smarty Jones—came home with us. My mom took Smarty to Florida. Woodrow stayed with me. Thus began the most durable love affair of my life.

It was not easy at first. Woodrow, like many puppies, was like Helen Keller pre–Annie Sullivan. He ravaged the apartment. He tore round and round in circles. He jumped on me, ceaselessly, while I tried to write, while I frantically googled "How to make puppy stop jumping." He ate a whole rawhide bone as big as his body in two minutes, causing me to then google "Can puppy die from eating whole rawhide?" One weekend I called Andy, who was in New Hampshire with his son, in tears. I said, "I feel like I'm babysitting somebody else's monster child. I don't want him. There's something wrong with him. Let's take him back."

But Woodrow, though willful, was supersmart, and once he realized I was also stubborn and, as the human, at least nominally the alpha, he gave in and grudgingly let me train him. He came. He sat. He dragged me up and down the ice-covered slopes of Beacon Hill several times a day, back and forth to the dog park on the Common, strangulating himself to get to the joyous open space. In the summer, as he grew, we started running by the Charles, Woodrow a few paces ahead of me—a dog's walking pace is a human's jogging one—the tips of his ears jauntily flapping. And although we had agreed not to let Woodrow on any of the furniture! Never! Ever! Especially on the bed!, one afternoon Andy came home from work and caught me napping with Woodrow next to me, the dog's head on my pillow. The look Andy gave us could not have been more gravely disappointed if he had caught me with another man.

Over the next several years, many things happened. I published that first book. I went on tour. It was successful. We moved out of the postage-stamp apartment on Beacon Hill and into a bigger place across the Public Garden in the Back Bay. There was another novel. Another tour. Another teaching job. Andy and I split up. There was another boyfriend, then another—the men came and went, like the women in the room in T. S. Eliot's "The Love Song of J. Alfred Prufrock." Woodrow, however, did not go. While everything else changed, and went, he stayed.

He was my structure and my laughter, my companion and travel partner, my responsibility and my daily joy. I was aware, on some level, that it was perhaps not the brightest move to invest all my emotional eggs in one basket, that basket being a canine who, unlike a human child, would not outlive me. Who would, in fact, almost certainly predecease me. I tried to ignore that every year for a human is seven for a dog, that when Woodrow turned six he was really forty-two, and when he turned eight, he was fifty-six. I was affronted that year to learn he was then considered a senior dog. And when he was ten, I found my first evidence of that: I was applying his flea and tick medication on his back when I saw, while ruffling the thick black fur on his spine, a single white hair. A clang of alarm sounded in me, distant but distinct. I had lost my dad, so I knew what that sound was: the warning of mortality. I smoothed Woodrow's fur back down, hiding the hair. "Never mind, Kooks," I said, using my nonsensical nickname for him—has any dog ever been consistently called by his real name? "We won't tell anybody. It'll be the secret hair."

More secret white hairs popped up over the next few years, in Woodrow's ears, between his toes, on his belly. Then they became not so secret. His back legs stiffened, as happens to so many Labs. He started taking a whole medicine cabinet of pills for arthritis, got acupuncture from a mobile vet as if he were Californian. He became unable to get up the stairs to my sleeping loft, so for the first time since he was a puppy, we slept apart. Some days I stood in the shower and cried because I knew I would lose him. Stop it, I'd tell myself, he's right here! Don't waste your time mourning him when he's still with you. And don't let him see you crying. I'd get out of the shower, towel off, smile at Woodrow lying on the bathroom rug, mindful not to slip on the tennis ball he'd ejected near my feet. He'd look fixedly at it: *There is a BALL, Mommoo. There is no time for foolish human sentiment.* "You're right, Kooks," I'd say. "I am here and you are here, and it is a good day."

The year Woodrow turned thirteen I lost my mom as well, to breast cancer. Her death was like a tsunami I saw coming toward me as I stood on shore, knowing it would roll over me and destroy many things and that I was helpless to stop it. I also knew I would surface eventually in its wake, flailing and choking amid the debris of my formerly recognizable life, and rebuild. I wasn't so sure about Woodrow's departure. I loved my mom, with the primal love of a young animal for its mother. And we were friends. And I saw her three or four times a year, talked to her once or twice a week. Woodrow was my mainstay. I didn't really regret not having children; I felt wistful about it sometimes, wishing I could have met the person my body would have made, but it had never been something I yearned for in my life plan. I had wanted a great love. And I had wanted to write books. In the latter, mercifully, I had succeeded, and if I was still looking for my forever partner, that was okay: I was rich in friends, I had a miraculous career, I had a full and wondrous life. Most of the time, I was happy with my choices.

But much of my happiness, and my stability, was predicated on my old dog. And if my mom's death was a tsunami, when I thought about Woodrow crossing the river, I thought of heading toward Niagara Falls in a barrel: the inevitability, the precipitous drop. I wasn't at all sure I would survive it.

This is what happened.

Drive-bys

Growing up I read, mostly in my mother's Judith Krantz novels, about women who could stop traffic simply by stepping into the street. These heroines do not live in Boston. If I try to cross Commonwealth Avenue at the wrong time or emerge from between parked cars instead of using the crosswalk, there's an excellent chance I'll be mowed over. Usually by somebody in a BMW, which I have long since decided—forgive me, Beamer drivers—is an acronym for *asshole*.

But that is before I discover my secret weapon: Woodrow. Not young Woodrow, whom drivers were equally happy to squash like a cartoon character beside me, but old Woodrow, limping across the street in his harness. The first time his legs give out, we are in fact in the middle of Commonwealth Avenue. Commonwealth is a major Boston thoroughfare, and drivers are always trying to catch all the green lights. Our block is especially bad, as it feeds onto Storrow Drive, Boston's answer to the West Side Highway, so people drive at high speeds and in high tempers. We are running this gauntlet to get to the Mall in a human-canine game of *Frogger*, as we do every day, when suddenly, for no reason, Woodrow sinks to the pavement. He looks up at me, scared: *Mommoo, what's happening to me?* "It's okay, Kooks," I say, straining to pick him up before the light turns.

"Just help me out here. Let's get out of the street, huh?" But Woodrow can't move.

The light changes. It's like a starting gun goes off. Traffic hurtles toward us . . . and screeches to a stop. I brace myself for a barrage of insults and profanity—I'm stooped over with my arms encircling Woodrow's belly, trying to lift and maneuver him to safety. A man does yell out of his window: "Hey! You need some help there?"

That's how it always is with Woodrow. I make every effort to ensure Commonwealth is clear before we cross, but sometimes Woodrow is extra slow, or people barrel off Storrow Drive, and then we are in the way. Yet in a city whose mouthy drivers would put New Jersey to shame, people call encouragement: *You go, dog! You got this!* Or: *How old's the pooch?* Sometimes, if the light's red and they're stuck in traffic, drivers will yell narratives to me through their windows about their own geriatric dogs, Duke, Scout, Pedro, all at home.

One morning I am helping Woodrow inside after a bench sit. It's one of his bad days; he's lurching forward like Captain Ahab on the foredeck. I grip his harness with both hands and call "Thank you!" to the drivers who are patiently waiting. They lift their fingers from their steering wheels or look up from their smartphones to give me a nod.

Once we've reached the sidewalk, I turn back again to wave and find one guy still sitting there in his truck. The light is green, so he could go; people are honking at him, swearing, swerving around him into the free lane. He's watching us, me and Woodrow, and I realize he's waiting for us to get safely inside. When I reach our building's front door, he salutes us and yells, "What you're doing with your dog, it's a great thing! You can see how much he loves you. It's a beautiful thing. Beautiful."

May

NEVER GIVE IN

I t was a good day, that Monday of Memorial Day weekend. May in Boston often feels like a party, people surg-
ing out after the long, salty gray winter to congregate in
the Common, the outdoor cafés lining Newbury Street.
And this day was particularly splendid. The sky was bright
blue, the cherry blossoms candy-pink. The tree my neighbors had planted thirty years ago outside my apartment
was so ridiculous with blooms that people had been taking
photos beneath it all week: engagement, prom, family por-
trait, so many that Jim, my photographer friend who was
visiting, had started taking photos of people taking photos
under the tree. The flowers were just starting to come off
and spiral downward, and Woodrow tried to snap them
out of the air like treats. He was feeling the good weather,
too. Every day we walked these historical sidewalks, as
we had since he'd been a baby puppy and I'd dragged him
along the bricks on his stomach. As a young adult he'd developed a gangster strut, shooting his front legs out as he
patrolled his hood. Now, as an elder statesman, he moved

with slow dignity and the aid of a harness, a contraption called a Help 'Em Up that allowed me to support his back legs. Did it bother him? Not a bit.

Today Woodrow took us on his regular route up the Commonwealth Mall to the Public Garden, where he rested amid the waist-high tulips for a while, his tongue lolling out as hot pink as the petals. He lapped at the fountains he used to jump into until the park rangers made me haul him out. He performance-bombed the Berklee College of Music trio playing a string rendition of "Don't Stop Believin'," and he greeted strangers with ambassadorial savoir faire, allowing out-of-towners who'd left their dogs at home to get their fix. *Oh, he looks just like our Buddy! How old? Fourteen? Wow! He's doing great for an old guy!* Woodrow accepted these compliments as his due. They were true, too: his muzzle was almost completely covered with what we called George Clooney gray, his teeth leaned every which way like the tombstones in the Old Granary Burying Ground, and his claws curved out in talons. But he still loved his food—especially bacon and carrots, which he extracted five at a time from the refrigerator crisper drawer. He loved his toys. He loved the ladies. And today the sun or the convivial crowd must have given him an extra jolt of energy, for he stumped straight through the Garden to the Common, where he planted himself in front of the hot dog cart and stared meaningfully at it until I got him not one, not two, but three footlongs.

This was what I attributed his lethargic pace to on the way home—that and the stop we'd made at the Frosty Ice Cream truck, where Woodrow ate a child cone in one T-Rex gulp, and also the Taj Hotel, where he finagled his usual Milk-Bones from the doormen. These days, I indulged Woodrow whenever he showed extra initiative. He was ninety-eight in human years—what harm would a few more treats do? But now he stopped every few steps, lying on the sidewalk and refusing to move. Even the water Jim poured into his hand for Woodrow to lick didn't help. "Maybe we shouldn't have given him the Frosty cone," I said as we finally reached our block.

"I don't think it's his stomach that's bothering him," said Jim. Jim was my former fiancé and had been Woodrow's dog dad for the second half of Woodrow's life; he was still beloved to us both, and he knew Woodrow almost as well as I did. "I think he's having trouble with his breathing," Jim said. "Can you hear it?"

"Oh, yeah, he always breathes like that when it's this hot," I said, although Woodrow did sound a little more like Darth Vader than usual. "It's a side effect of getting old, like his old-man gag."

On cue, Woodrow produced a noise like something caught in a garbage disposal, half choke, half retch. "Good one, Kooks," I said. This was the sound that woke me, my alarm clock every morning, from Woodrow's bed beneath my sleeping loft.

"I don't know," Jim said. "I don't think his breathing sounds normal. Listen."

I did. We'd reached my building by then and were in the lobby at the foot of the stairs, sixteen of them, which Woodrow took slowly and with assistance. Jim was right. This wasn't the usual panting of exertion. Woodrow paused and gagged on each step, head down, sides heaving. There was foam on his muzzle. I looked at Jim in alarm.

"Think we should run him to the vet?" I said.

"Let's record it and send it in," he suggested. Jim was a *National Geographic* and Nikon photographer, and his response to most situations was to document them.

"Good idea," I said.

We got Woodrow settled in his favorite spot, his sheepskin in front of my bay windows. Blossoms from the cherry tree showered down like pink snow while I recorded Woodrow on my iPhone. Now that we were inside, away from the street noise, I could hear his lungs rumbling as if they had a bike chain in them. A death rattle, my grandmother Luverne would have called it; she'd had one herself, when she had pneumonia. I sent the recording to Dr. Mimi, Woodrow's mobile vet and acupuncturist. I'm so sorry to bother you on a holiday weekend, I texted, but does Woodrow's breathing sound bad to you?

The three little dots rippled, telling me Dr. Mimi was reading and typing. I'd take him to South Bay, she wrote. Get a chest x-ray.

"Okay," I said and stood up. "Who wants to go for a ride?"

Rather than waste time on the stairs, Jim picked Woodrow up and carried him out to my Jeep, where he deposited him in the back seat—Woodrow's lifelong territory. "Guess what, Kooks," I said, "we're going to see some ladies!" Woodrow loved the vet, where there were other dogs, treats that sometimes included Easy Cheese on tongue depressors, and female doctors.

At South Bay Vet, the tech hurried us into an exam room. Woodrow gagged and retched while Dr. Gardiner examined him. He looked hopefully at the treat jar when she was done, but she was frowning. "I can't tell without an X-ray," she said, "but I think his heart is dangerously enlarged. I'd take him to the Angell."

Every pet owner in Boston knew Angell Animal Medical Center; it was for emergency treatment. "Okay," I said. "So we'll wait for you to do the X-ray and . . ."

"I'll call and let them know you're coming," Dr. Gardiner said. "You need to go *now*."

Back outside I drove as quickly as I dared through streets thronged with people enjoying the day, petals everywhere like ticker tape, a party we were no longer attending. "Hold on, Kooks," I said to Woodrow, who was panting heavily between rounds of sniffs out the window. "We're going to the nice Angell to see even more ladies! It's going to be so good."

At the hospital a tech was waiting to lead Woodrow through the reception lounge to the double doors, beyond which was the hospital where civilians could rarely go. "See you soon, buddy," Jim said as Woodrow limped away, gagging. "We'll be right here," I called.

Then came the hard part. We waited. Jim, more sociable than I in emergency situations, made friends with all the other owners and their animals like the Doctor Dolittle he was, while I sat on a blond wood bench and watched the flatscreen photo display of dogs, cats, birds, and reptiles the Angell had successfully treated. Whenever the double doors opened, everyone looked up with a mixture of anticipation and fear. Nobody wanted to be the kind of pet owner you occasionally saw at Angell, people who'd been summoned back behind those doors and stumbled out again holding only a leash, their faces destroyed by grief. That would be all of us someday. It was inevitable. *But please, God, not yet*, I prayed. I wasn't religious, but as on turbulent flights, there were no atheists in emergency rooms. I sent up my ragged but heartfelt writer girl prayers. *Please, not Woodrow. Not today.*

The double doors opened and a young female tech came out with Woodrow. "Jenna with Woodrow?" she called.

"Here," I said.

Jim got down on the linoleum with Woodrow while the tech drew me aside. "So Woodrow was going into heart failure," she said. "It's a good thing you got him in when

you did. We put him in an oxygen tent, and he did stabi-
lize. So we think he's okay to go home."

"Thank God," I said. I suddenly felt numb. "So he'll be
okay?"

"Well," she said carefully, "he is of very advanced age, as
you know."

She handed me a gallon baggie full of prescription bot-
tles and a sheaf of printed handouts. "These are his meds,"
she said. "They should help get him more comfortable.
Keep him as calm and quiet as possible. Call us if you have
any questions, and monitor his breathing. If it gets worse
again, let us know right away."

I glanced at the information sheets in my hand. Sildenafil. Pimobendan. Levothyroxine. Woodrow already took
phenobarbital for seizures, gabapentin and Previcox for
pain. He would be a walking pharmacy. "Thank you," I said.

I checked out at the front desk, handing over my credit
card for an amount that would have bought me a small car.
Woodrow sat next to my feet. He was still panting, but the
gagging had stopped and he looked with interest, perking
his ears, at the other dogs waiting to be seen. "Did you
have fun in there, you expensive old man?" I asked, and
Woodrow gave me the side-eye. *Of course I did, Mommoo.*
There were ladies. We left the hospital, and as we stepped
into the parking lot, I felt as triumphant as though I were
leading a parade.

Jim was lifting Woodrow into the Jeep when I heard

someone calling my name. A dark, handsome man in scrubs came jogging out of the hospital. "I'm Dr. Zarin," he said. "I wanted to catch you before you left, to be sure you understood Woodrow's condition."

"That's kind of you," I said, puzzled. It seemed above and beyond to me that the doctor should chase us out into the parking lot to make sure we were well informed, but the Angell had always provided excellent service.

Dr. Zarin produced another stack of printouts, which he set on the hood of the Jeep. Jim and I stood on either side of him as the doctor took out a pen, underlining things here, drawing diagrams there. I tried to concentrate; I was a science geek and normally loved this kind of stuff. But Dr. Zarin's explanations, the words he was using—cardiomyopathy, pulmonary edema, hypertension—slid off my brain.

"So bottom line," Dr. Zarin said, putting his pen away, "is there's no cure for Woodrow's condition. The medication may help for a while, but sooner rather than later, you should be prepared to make that difficult decision."

I nodded. I found myself squinting, which was what I always did when trying to process the incomprehensible. "Just so I'm completely clear," I said, "what is Woodrow's condition?"

"Congestive heart failure," Dr. Zarin said.

"And can you tell me . . . how long is sooner than later?"

Dr. Zarin looked at me sadly.

"I know you can't be specific," I added. My mom's diagnosis had taught me that. "But maybe a ballpark estimate?"

"It's about quality of life," he said. "You'll know when the time comes."

I nodded again and looked into the back seat, where Woodrow panted heavily, glancing from me to Jim to Dr. Zarin. I now realized why the doctor had come out to the parking lot: he hadn't wanted us to be inside among other people while he delivered, in the gentlest way possible, Woodrow's death sentence. "Thank you," I said.

"Yes, thank you," said Jim. The two men talked a little more while I got in behind the steering wheel and shut the door. I looked through the windshield at the clouds above the parking lot, gold and pink. I thought of my parents somewhere up there, in the heaven they didn't believe in, and how ever since my mom was nine years old, when she lugged home her first stray, Spunky, she'd never gone a year without a dog; how my dad's dogs were, in addition to his kids, the chief pleasure of his life. How many times I had seen him fly past our kitchen window, pulled by our team of Labs, his arms hyperextended as they dragged him joyously down the street. "Heel," he bellowed ineffectually. "HEEL!" "You magnificent creatures," he murmured to them, scratching their ears, as they dozed. I asked my parents, silently, to get ready for Woodrow, to prepare to receive him and take good care of him when he, too, crossed that big river. Woodrow panted meanwhile, his mollusk breath filling the car.

Finally Jim got in. "You okay?" he asked. I shook my head. Tears filled my eyes, but I gripped the steering wheel. I did not want Woodrow to hear or see me cry. Jim put his hand on the back of my neck.

When I had myself under control, I turned to Woodrow, who was staring happily at us with his black round-button eyes: he was in the car with his people, he was leaving the scary place, everything was okay. My good dog! What had he ever done to harm anyone? I reached back between the seats to pat his head as I'd done thousands of times before. "You ready, Kooks?" I said. "Let's go home."

Like most Labs, Woodrow had had his share of near-death experiences. His first came before he was a year old: we were visiting Andy's parents in New Hampshire. I'd warned them before we left Boston to put away anything that was food, looked like food, or could be mistaken for food, but since they had a Newfoundland and a German shepherd, dogs with normal appetites, they didn't take me seriously. After the visit, on the drive home, I commented, "Wow, Woodrow's growing so fast—look how big his rib cage is! Even his belly looks twice as big." At our apartment, when I set Woodrow's dinner bowl on the floor, he backed away. The first rule of Lab ownership is: if a Lab doesn't eat, he's dying. That was Woodrow's first trip to the Angell, where they pumped his stomach, put him on an IV, and lectured me on taking him to a place where people had left a garbage can full of kibble unguarded in the garage.

When he was four, Woodrow was playing in a park in the Fells, a wooded area north of Boston, when he clocked heads with another dog who was going for the same toy. The sound their skulls made was like two pool balls smacking together. Seconds later, Woodrow was thrashing and convulsing on the ground. Somehow we carried him the three miles out of the woods to my friend Kirsten's car, and back we went to the Angell. Woodrow was permanently prone to seizures after that, infrequent but grand mal, each lasting a potentially fatal five or more minutes. I had syringes preloaded with diazepam to inject Woodrow with and stop a seizure in progress—"Why can't somebody shoot Valium up my butt?" my friend Julie asked plaintively, when she heard about this. And twice a day, Woodrow got his Don Draper drug: a tiny tab of phenobarbital.

The most threatening incident was also the most peculiar. While my mom was sick, in the final stages of her breast cancer, I was in Florida helping take care of her while Woodrow stayed in Minnesota, at my family house with Jim. One afternoon Jim called me: "Honey," he said, "I hate to trouble you with this, but I think there's something wrong with Woodrow's eyes." What do you mean? I asked. Jim texted me a photo that showed Woodrow's eyes not only bulging out of his head but pointing in different directions. He looked like a thyroidal pug, or a creature from Stephen King's *Pet Sematary*, run over by a car and put back together the wrong way. Jim had taken him to the vet and even to a canine ophthalmologist, but although Woodrow had dangerous pressure buildup in his eyes, nobody could determine the cause. It wasn't the usual suspect, glaucoma. Drops hadn't helped. "I'm so sorry to tell you this," said the vet when she called to fill me in, "especially because I know what you're going through with your mom. But there's a good chance Woodrow has a brain tumor."

So the week after my mom passed away, I found myself driving across the frozen landscape of Minnesota with my thirteen-year-old Lab in the back seat. I took him to Blue Pearl in Minneapolis, a specialty clinic, for an MRI. If Woodrow survived that—no guarantee, since putting such an old dog under general anesthesia was risky—we'd see whether he had a tumor. If he had a tumor, well . . . checkmate. Chemo for dogs often isn't as invasive as chemo for humans, but Woodrow would have to be knocked out every time he received it, and he was just too old. When discussing my options with me, the vet had let the sentence dangle in a way I'd become familiar with from talking to my mom's oncologist. *If that's the scenario, well . . .*

I turned Woodrow over to the Blue Pearl vet techs and sat in the waiting room with my muddy boots and iPhone. My friends texted me encouraging Bitmojis, videos of their lit candles and Tibetan bowls ringing, GIFs of Arnold Schwarzenegger saying "IT'S NOT A TOOMAH." I sent up my amateur prayers: *Please God, not Woodrow, too. Not now. Please just let me have him a little longer. Just one more year.* I could not, I felt, be the woman who lost her mom and her dog within days of each other. My overall view of the universe was that, like Dr. Martin Luther King's moral arc, it was long but bent ultimately toward good. If Woodrow died that day, I would have to revise that opinion. I kept thinking of the previous year, when my mom had a stroke after her last round of chemo. In her hospital in Florida, I'd sat with her and watched her, this tiny bald woman with no eyelashes or brows, a concert pianist, trying like hell to touch the fingers and thumb of her right hand together. For all our vanity, our hairstyling and pedicures and Botox and pretty clothes, this, this moment, was true beauty. I had flown back from that trip and sat on the floor of my study with Woodrow, who was getting so old and gray, and literally howled my fear and outrage. I could not lose my mom and my dog in the same week.

After a few hours, the doctor came to fetch me. Woodrow had survived the MRI, and he had no tumor. Stoic throughout the wait, as dry-eyed as I'd been ever since my mom died, I now burst into tears. "I'm sorry," I sobbed.

"I'm just so relieved." The neurosurgeon nodded understandingly, but she was distracted.

"I still have no idea what's causing the ocular pressure," she said. "Do you want to see his scans?" I did. I followed her back into the hospital, where on a computer screen she pulled up a cross-section of what looked like a walnut. My dog's brain, halved and exposed. "Beautiful," the doctor said, scowling. "Not a thing wrong with it. This is the kind of puzzle that drives doctors crazy."

Woodrow spent a woozy hour with me in an exam room while the anesthetic wore off, smiling at the nurses who checked his vitals and trying to stagger out the door. He had a monk's patch on the back of his head where they'd shaved him for the MRI. One eye still looked into one corner of the room; the other pointed at the wall. On the way home, after the techs helped me lift him into the Jeep, I swung through a Starbucks drive-through to get him a Puppy Whip, a child's cup full of whipped cream, and when I got him back to my family house, Jim and I fried up the whole pound of bacon we'd promised Woodrow if he survived the procedure. He ate all of it, and the next morning his eyes were back to normal. Round, black, alert, their surfaces only slightly convex. Shining at me as if to say, *I made my eyes bulge out of my head and then pulled them back in again, Mommoo, HAHAHA! Wasn't that so funny?* "Very funny, Kooks," I said. There was also a glint beneath the mischief, an expression that might or might not

have said, *I knew you were sad, so I manufactured a distraction.*
I wouldn't have put it past him. Or it might have been my
mom, causing the pressure in Woodrow's eyes and then
retracting it, so that instead of pure grief, I felt gratitude. I
wouldn't have put it past her, either. Whatever the cause,
whoever did it and then cured it, somebody saved Woodrow that day.

When we got back from the Angell, I thought Woodrow
would be tired and want to go lie on his sheepskin in front
of the bay windows, or at least get five or six carrots from
his crisper drawer. Instead, he wanted to go to his bench
on the Mall. We visited the bench every day, morning and
evening, so Woodrow could flop down in the dirt patch
his body had made in the grass and preside over his kingdom. Watch birds and squirrels—especially his favorite,
the rare white squirrel I'd nicknamed Sauvignon Blanca.
Greet his human and canine admirers. Sniff the air.

We sat on the bench for a while under the big trees,
cottonwoods and oaks. Traffic and people passed. Many
smiled. A few stopped to pet Woodrow. *How old? Fourteen!*
Wow! Woodrow gazed regally into the distance as if nothing unusual had happened that day. He was not gagging;
his breathing seemed fine. I read the information sheet
about Woodrow's medication and condition: *Congestive*
Heart Failure and Your Dog. Jim smoked a cigar. Suddenly

Woodrow levered himself up and started limping off down the Mall, trailing the straps of his harness.

"Kooks!" I said, jumping up. "Where are you going?"

"Wait for us, buddy," Jim called.

Woodrow stumped along as determinedly as any old sailor heading toward a bar after several years at sea. I caught up with him and grabbed his harness handle just before he walked into the traffic on Berkeley Street. It was unbelievable, but my old boy, who'd been in the ER not an hour ago, was taking us back toward the Public Garden—and the Taj.

The Taj, aka the Ritz to old-school Bostonians, faced the Garden on Arlington Street, Boston's version of the Plaza. Every day Woodrow took me there, even if I was still in my pajamas or had no makeup on, to say hello to the senators, European travelers, wedding parties, and well-coiffed residents. And his favorites, the doormen. Tommy and Leslie, Woodrow's friends who stood beneath the grand awning all year in their uniforms and white gloves and, in addition to hailing cabs and hauling luggage carts, handed out treats from a Tupperware tub they kept hidden behind a gold-and-black lacquered door. Today it was Tommy who greeted us as Woodrow pitched toward him, dragging his harness and leash.

"How you doing, old-timer?" Tommy said, opening the secret cabinet, which also contained extra flashlights, whistles, umbrellas, and, at Christmas, the fifth of Glenlivet I gave them. "We hadn't seen you in a couple of days. We were getting worried."

Woodrow snapped the Milk-Bone Tommy tossed him out of midair. Woodrow might have had cataracts, but when it came to catching treats, he had batlike sonar. "We had a little adventure today," I said. "We had to go to the Angell."

"Oh yeah?" Tommy said, glancing at me from beneath the brim of his cap. He knew what the Angell was. He had a boxer pup at home. "What'd you do, buddy," he said to Woodrow, "you give your mama a scare?"

"He had some heart trouble," I said, "but he's okay now."

"Of course he is," said Tommy. "I know what your trouble is, old guy. Your heart's just too big." He winked at me, apparently unaware of how accurate his words were, and threw Woodrow several more Milk-Bones. Tommy knew two things from experience: if he fed Woodrow from his hand, he might lose a finger to Woodrow's enthusiasm and dim eyesight. And if he gave Woodrow only one treat, Woodrow would slide down onto his stomach on the Taj red carpet, blocking the revolving door and all the guests going in or out, until he had received his fair due.

"Who's a piece a work?" said Tommy to Woodrow, who thumped his tail once: *I am, obviously.* "All right, one more. Now go with Mama."

He handed me a treat so I could lure Woodrow away

and held up his gloved palms to prove to Woodrow he had no more. "Thanks, Tommy," I said. "See you tomorrow."

"Hope so," said Tommy. "Take care, sweetheart."

I started moonwalking backward along Arlington Street, Woodrow shuffling toward the treat in my outstretched hand. As we made our slow way home, drivers honking and yelling, "Get it, dog!" and "You can do it!," I thought there were probably plenty among them who'd say what I'd done today was foolish. The race to the vet, the ER; forking over a couple of mortgage payments to keep alive a dog who was destined not to last much longer anyway. Labs typically live to be eleven, twelve, and that is considered old. Woodrow was fourteen. He was basically Methuselah. He'd had so many health struggles, and now he would have more. His medications would have side effects. They were expensive. And they were palliative: if you believed Dr. Zarin, they would not help Woodrow get better. I remembered one morning in the last week of my mom's life, making French toast with ice cream and vanilla frosting, anything to convince her to eat, and realizing that there was nothing I could cook for her, nothing I could do, that would cure her. There were a lot of people, I suspected, who, faced with Woodrow's crisis today, would have let him go. Who might have put him down when he started having trouble with stairs. Enough is enough, they might have said. He's had a good life.

But I was stubborn. I'd inherited the trait along with my love of Labs: my dad's family had survived pogroms; my mom's had pioneered in rural Minnesota. Both parents said that if they told me to breathe, I'd hold my breath until I'd turn blue. And I loved attempting the impossible. If you told me something couldn't be done, I wanted to do it all the more. So many well-meaning people had advised me—my parents, thank God, not among them—that it wasn't possible to earn a living writing books. I should do something practical. I had thanked them, then gone on to make a career out of it. I had a Winston Churchill quote on the wall above my desk: *Never give in, never give in, never give in.* Whatever I loved, I fought for. And there was nothing I loved more than Woodrow.

Woodrow had some of that indomitable spirit as well. An hour earlier, he'd been in an oxygen tent. Now he was drawing applause from passing cars. When he'd started having trouble walking, Dr. Mimi had given me a quality-of-life calculator designed to help people decide when it was time to put their pets down. It asked questions about various areas of the pet's life—appetite, mobility, continence, comfort—and assigned numerical values to the answers. A low score—8 was the lowest—meant your pet was suffering and it was time. The highest score, 80, meant your pet was in prime health. Woodrow had recently scored a 35. As far as his time was concerned, I would use the calculator—and

I would go by the rule one of my favorite authors, Anna Quindlen, had applied to her own old dog: As long as the nose and tail still work . . . the dog is happy.

In a movie my mom and I loved, *Shining Through*, based on the Susan Isaacs novel of the same name, the heroine, a New York spy in Berlin fighting the Nazis, asks her contact, a fishmonger, for information about her Jewish cousins in hiding. The fishmonger slaps fish down on the table in front of her: one, two, three, each representing one of her relatives. "They have tremendous fight, these fish," he says, eyes shining. "Three times the net has swept over them. Three times they have escaped." Today, by some miracle, I had not left the Angell empty-handed. Here was Woodrow walking toward me. The net had swept over him again.

Quality-of-Life Scale Calculator

Adapted from www.journeyspet.com

Instructions: For each variable there is a value of 10 points, with an example for scores of 1, 5, and 10 as guidance. Use your judgment to decide how your pet scores. For example, under "Eating and Drinking," if your pet eats only treats, you may assign a value of 2 or 3—higher than 1, not eating at all, but less than 5, your pet eating slightly less of his regular food than is normal.

JUMPING OR MOBILITY

1 point: Your pet cannot walk or stand without assistance.

5 points: Your pet can move around as long as she has her pain medication. She can do about half the activities she did when she was healthier, get half the distance on a walk, or spend half the time doing activities (chasing a Frisbee, swimming, hunting).

10 points: Your pet is fully active and enjoying all her activities.

OUCH OR PAIN

1 point: Your pet seems in pain (whining, crying, not willing to move) even while taking pain medication. (Note: many animals will hide pain or weakness as a survival trait.)

5 points: Your pet is on pain medications, and they are helping at least 75 percent of the time.

10 points: Your pet is pain-free.

UNCERTAINTY AND UNDERSTANDING (OF CONDITION)

1 point: Your pet has a medical diagnosis that cannot be predicted. The problem may present in sudden, catastrophic events.

5 points: Your pet has a medical condition that can change over time, but it is currently stable, and you are able to monitor it (with the help of your veterinarian) and make adjustments when necessary. You understand what to watch for, the treatment plan, and when your pet needs medical attention.

10 points: Your pet is happy and healthy; there are no medical issues beyond routine preventive care.

RESPIRATION OR BREATHING

1 point: Your pet has severe episodes of difficulty breathing, coughing, or open-mouthed breathing. Your pet is not eating or drinking in an effort to breathe. At this point you should seek immediate medical attention for your pet.

5 points: Your pet has occasional bouts of coughing, wheezing, or exercise intolerance. These are short (less than 2 minutes), and your pet is on prescribed medication that can be adjusted to help.

10 points: Your pet has no coughing, wheezing, or exercise intolerance.

NEATNESS OR HYGIENE

1 point: Your pet spends time lying in his waste. He may be unable to control his elimination, or be unable to move after elimination. He may have an external tumor or mass that you are unable to keep clean and/or bandaged. Your pet may have pressure sores (bed sores) from lying down and being unable to move.

5 points: Your pet may need assistance to eliminate, but he does not spend time lying in his waste. He is able to hold his waste until he gets assistance. He may have an external tumor or mass, but it can be kept clean and/or bandaged, and it is not infected. Your pet may groom himself, but may need assistance in some areas.

10 points: Your pet can eliminate waste and groom without assistance. He has no medical issues that are causing him to have a bad odor. You can provide any care issues to address his hygiene (baths, trip to the groomer, teeth cleaning, etc.).

EATING AND DRINKING

1 point: Your pet is refusing food and water. She may be vomiting or have diarrhea (or both). She may be nauseous. Cats may "hang out" at the water bowl, next to it, or with their heads hanging over it.

5 points: Your pet is eating more slowly, and is not as interested in food as she used to be. She may go back several times before she finishes a meal. She is eating slightly less than usual, but is eating her regular food.

10 points: Your pet is eating and drinking normally.

YOU

1 point: You are constantly worried about your pet. You may not understand what is happening to him medically. You feel overwhelmed and stressed trying to provide for his needs, physically, emotionally, or financially, or unable to provide for him at all. You may be worried about how he will fare when you are away on an upcoming trip. There may be tension in the family and disagreement on how to proceed.

5 points: You understand your pet's condition, and are able, with some effort, to meet his needs. You may have concerns, but they are manageable.

10 points: You are easily able to meet your pet's needs, and not worried about any aspect of his care.

SOCIAL ABILITY

1 point: Your pet does not spend time with the family. She may hide, become irritable, or snap if bothered. Some pets that do not enjoy being petted may not seem to care if they are petted. Perhaps your pet is unable physically to get to the room where she usually spends time with others.

5 points: Your pet spends at least half the time with the family. She is not irritable or snippy. She happily greets you when you come home.

10 points: Your pet enjoys you, the family, and others (including other animals she may know), greets you at the door when you arrive home, and seeks out company.

JOURNEYS QUALITY-OF-LIFE SCALE—TOTAL

There are no hard-and-fast rules, although in general a higher score is better.

- A score of 80 is a happy, healthy pet!
- A score of 8 is a pet that is suffering. A low score on any of the measures may be a reason to consider euthanasia.

We hope this was a helpful starting place to explore your pet's quality of life, and address your concerns with your veterinarian.

Housekeeping

Every Monday morning, a housekeeping crew comes to clean our building, hired and supervised by John, our maintenance guy. I feel a little bad about this, elitist before the word became a catch-phrase. When I first moved into my building in the Back Bay, I volunteered to clean it myself, vacuuming the red Oriental carpets and polishing the brass chandeliers and doorknobs, buffing the marble stairs. I like cleaning, I said; it's my favorite form of procrastination, and it'd be a good workout. And it would save the condo association money! But I was laughed out of the meeting. The building is really too big a job for one person to handle, the cotrustees told me, and besides, it would never do. The implication: This is the Back Bay, baby, and ever since landfill was hauled in to create the neighborhood atop Boston Harbor and the nouveau riche mansions built upon it, the elegant residences have always been tended by chimney sweeps (our building still uses such a service), ironmongers, gardeners, and housekeepers. This is the way it has always been done. This is how it'll continue to be.

So every Monday I say hi to our housekeeping crew, two Latina ladies in jeans and T-shirts, better dressed than I am. I offer them coffee and water, which they politely decline, and leave cookies and doughnuts on the foyer console, and we get to know one another in the weirdly distant yet intimate way people do when their lives intersect behind the scenes. The ladies have seen me doing laundry and putting out garbage in my underwear; I have seen them windexing the window panels and hauling an industrial Electrolux up three flights of stairs. (Our grande dame of a building, constructed in 1860, has no elevator.) We talk about upcoming holidays; they tell me how their children are, the misbehavior of their husbands, ex-husbands, and boyfriends. They are unfailingly nice to Woodrow, even when he walks on the freshly mopped floors. "Hey, baby," they croon to him, "hi, handsome. How are you doing?" Of course, Woodrow loves them—his Monday ladies! They are a high point of his week. They bring treats for him, take out their smartphones to show me the antics of their own dogs, a mutt, a Pekingese.

One morning they are already hard at work, per usual, when I help Woodrow limp down the stairs. As always seems to happen when it's time for him to go out, the steps are newly clean, still glistening with soap and polish. The lady at the foot of the stairs, Beatriz, stops rubbing Brasso onto the door panel to watch our progress. "Do you need some help?" she says.

"No, we're okay, thank you," I say, as I help Woodrow across the lobby. He stops to wag at Beatriz.

"Hi, baby," she says, and stoops to pet him. She looks up at me with a stricken expression.

"He is breathing like . . . ," she says, and puts a hand on her heart, making a gasping noise. "Is he sick?"

"He was, but he has medicine, so he's better," I say. "He's just . . . old."

Beatriz straightens, suddenly businesslike again. "Ah," she says. "That is not an illness. That is a privilege," and she opens the door for us to go outside.

June

ASK FOR HELP

That night Jim and I went to bed with a sense of accomplishment. We had, after all, brought Woodrow back from the brink of death—with a little help from Drs. Mimi, Gardiner, and Zarin and the crews at South Bay and Angell. Woodrow had ingested his new medications with dinner and was sleeping peacefully. Every hour Jim had timed Woodrow's heart rate using his iPhone; it was fast, but, according to the *Congestive Heart Failure & Your Dog* information sheet, within normal range. We watched the big old muscle pumping along beneath the thin fur of Woodrow's rib cage. Finally we went to bed. "Good night, Kooks," I said, climbing up to the loft, "Mommoo loves you more than anyone in the universe. Yes, she does." I said this every night, and as I turned out the light, I had the feeling I often did when Woodrow was safely sleeping beneath me and I could hear his breathing and snores: *God's in his heaven, all's right with the world.*

In the middle of the night, though, I snapped awake. Jim was alert, too: "Did you hear something?" he asked me, as at the same time I turned to him and said, "What was that noise?" And then: "Do you . . . *smell* something weird?" I switched on the light and we peered over the side of the loft balcony into my study below, where Woodrow was shuttling back and forth in a panic, trying desperately to escape the stream shooting from under his tail: a police-hose blast of poop.

"Oh my God!" I said, scrambling out of bed. We raced downstairs. My study was like a murder scene, except with poop instead of blood. It was on Woodrow's bed, on my bookshelves, on the rugs, on my desk, even on the *walls*. Poor Woodrow was bug-eyed; since Day 1 of his puppy training at eight weeks, he had never, not once, had an accident in the house. Now he was frantic with fear: *What is HAPPENING to me?*

"Get a bowl!" I screamed to Jim, who had run to the kitchen, presumably for paper towels.

"What?" he shouted back.

"A bowl! Bring a bowl!" I yelled. Jim appeared in the doorway with a roll of Bounty and—the dish drainer.

"NOT the dish drainer!" I said. "A bowl! The big mixing bowl!" Jim looked dumbfounded at the dish drainer in his hand. "Never mind," I said, grabbing Woodrow's harness. "I'll get him outside."

"I'll bat cleanup," Jim yelled after us as I half carried, half dragged Woodrow from the apartment and down the building's stairs as fast as we could go, which wasn't very fast. We left a brown stream on every marble step, and in the lobby Woodrow released a puddle. His ears were back and he was licking his chops in fear. *I'm sorry, Mommoo.*

"It's okay, Kooks," I said. "It happens to everybody sometimes." This was what I always said when Woodrow had a vomit moment or showed a sign of his age: collapsing abruptly or bumping into a wall. But for once it was untrue. I had never seen anything like this.

Mercifully the night was warm, since I was in my sleep tank and underwear. I got Woodrow across the street to the Mall, where he limped back and forth, still expelling poop. Who knew the old boy had so much in him? How was it even possible? Jim came out to relieve me. "I did the best I could in there," he said.

He had, and it was a decent start. But there was just so much. I hauled Woodrow's bed into the bathtub and turned the shower on. I carried the rugs to the basement laundry room, where I shoved them into the deep sink and tossed in half a bottle of detergent. The sheepskin Woodrow slept on had to be junked; his toys, Stinky Chickie and his beloved stuffed hamburger and hot dog and avocado, went into the washing machine with bleach and a prayer. And yet when I returned upstairs with the building's mop and bucket, I saw: *But wait! There's more!* Every time I thought surely I'd gotten the last of it, I'd turn around and find a new splash on a wall, drawer, or door. I scrubbed and wiped and wrung, the whole time feeling panic and despair.

I'm a neat freak by nature, with no scatological sense of humor. I don't even like poop jokes. Now my apartment was an abattoir. Was this what our lives would become? How would I handle it? By the time I finished washing down the building's staircase and foyer—how had Woodrow gotten poop on the *mailboxes?*—and showered, it was almost dawn.

I made a nest of towels on the floor for Woodrow where his bed usually was and ran a towel over his belly, tail, paws, and rump, until it came back clean. I sat and petted him while he dozed off, depleted and exhausted, and called the Angell. "I think my dog's had a bad reaction to his medication," I said to the vet on duty, and described the Poopsplosion.

"That sounds like the pimobendan," she said.

"Should I take him off it?" I asked, "or give him a half-dose or something?"

"No," she said firmly. "This is the one medication we really need him to be on. It helps keep his heart contracting properly. Unfortunately it does sometimes have this side effect, but give him the full dosage."

"Side effect!" I said. "This isn't a side effect. It's a horror movie. Isn't this amount of diarrhea dangerous for him?"

"True, we don't want him to get dehydrated," she agreed. "If he's still this bad in forty-eight hours, bring him back in."

I thanked her, hung up, and dragged upstairs, where Jim, damp from his own shower, was back in bed. I recapped the conversation. "I don't know what I'm going to do," I said. I meant in general, but I also meant that day: I was due in New York for a superimportant audition with the Jewish Book Council for my latest novel, *The Lost Family*, which, if it went well, meant I'd tour with the JBC for the next several months. It was a coveted prize and privilege to be able to participate, and my publisher had already sent three hundred books to the council members, and my audition was in . . . eight hours.

"I can't leave Woodrow like this," I said. "What if he has another Poopsplosion? Or goes into heart failure?"

"I'll take care of him," Jim said. "Leave the car keys, and if I have to, I'll get him to the Angell."

"But what if there's an emergency and he . . . dies," I whispered, "and I'm not here? How would I ever forgive myself?"

There was no answer to this. I checked my phone: my train departed in three hours, more time than I'd slept. I had to get into a red dress, Spanx, and heels and onto a stage, and my feet were pruney, my hands cracked from bleach. The apartment reeked of it. Jim said, "You don't have to decide now. Maybe you can take a later train, reschedule the audition. You can call them in the morning."

"It *is* morning," I said. Daylight leached through the blinds. We lay in silence, listening with dread for more noises from downstairs.

A week later I lay with Woodrow on his sheepskin rug under my bay windows. Aside from getting him outside twice a day to do his business, a Herculean and exhausting venture, we hadn't moved much from this spot. Woodrow's breathing was quiet, his heartbeat regular, and thank merciful God, there had been no more Poopsplosions. The medications had saved his life. Their side effects had also shrunk it. Woodrow could barely walk; his balance was off, and he'd developed a Charlie Chaplin waddle, with a weird little flip-kick of his right rear leg. His appetance, one of those medical terms I wished I'd never had to learn, was down. He refused his regular food, his carrots from the crisper drawer—and this was a dog for whom, every time I went on a trip, I ordered twenty pounds of carrots from Instacart—and even the chicken and rice I'd made after the Poopsplosion. I'd been hand-feeding him anything he'd eat: human-grade chicken salad (he wouldn't touch it without celery and mayo), hamburger hot dish, mac and cheese so orange and congealed with extra Velveeta that I'd nicknamed it Donald Trump Blood. Mostly, Woodrow slept.

Jim had gone back to Minnesota that morning, unable to extend his visit any longer. "I hate to think of you trying to manage this alone," he'd said, as he got into his Uber. Me too, I thought but didn't say. I'd wished Jim a safe trip and gone back inside to the rug.

"Here, Kooks," I said now, holding a finger-full of the Trump Blood under Woodrow's sideways-comma nostrils. They quivered, and he opened one eye a slit. Without lifting his head, he lipped some of the macaroni off my finger. The rest fell to the rug. His eye closed again.

"Good boy," I said. I lay down with him, my head against his ribs. Outside, the last of the cherry blossoms spiraled from the tree, the new little green leaves shining. People walked past with their kids, dogs, iced coffees. I could hear them out there, talking, laughing, car radios thumping bass. I wished them well and shut my eyes.

I really didn't know how I was going to manage. I'd missed my audition for the Jewish Book Council, although my fierce, fabulous agent Stéphanie had gone to bat for me when I'd told her about Woodrow's health crisis, and they'd let me send in a video instead. I'd changed my shirt and slashed on some lipstick while Jim minded Woodrow, and my friend Sara, a yoga guru with her own Instagram empire, had helped me film. She'd also, the morning after the Poopsplosion, come over with plastic-backed drop cloths from Home Depot that she'd made a special trip to get for us, since I didn't dare leave Woodrow.

"Oh Baby Krishna," she said, seeing me through our building's glass door as I came through the lobby, in T-shirt and gym shorts, my hair in a messy bun. "You look so tired, Jennuschka. How is he?"

"Sleeping, for now." I cracked the door to let her pass me the drop cloths. "Thank you so much, Zaruschka. I'd invite you up, but believe me, you don't want to be there. Go now! Save yourself!" We'd both laughed, as if I were kidding.

Sara wasn't the only person who helped us that week. Social media, for all its flaws, was excellent for one thing: getting news to a lot of people quickly. When my mom passed, refusing any memorial, I'd posted her tribute on Facebook; it shocked and horrified so many people, because, I discovered belatedly, she hadn't let anyone know she was sick. Her friends were stunned in addition to devastated, and I didn't want Woodrow's followers—he had his own Facebook and Instagram accounts—to suffer the same way. So, although I deliberately cultivated a cheerful presence online, I went against my own rules and crafted a post about Woodrow's health scare.

So today our boy is home from MSPCA-Angell Animal Medical Center—which is above & beyond fantastic—with some new meds. His diagnosis is congestive heart failure, which is not a great thing at his age but can be managed with medication if we are lucky.

Thank you to our doctors, our friends, & as always the doormen at Taj Boston for bringing us back to life. 🐾 🙏 ♥

Woodrow's post was more pithy:

This is ME at the TAJ an hour after being in an "oxygen tent" & triumphing over "congestive heart failure" HAHAHA. Please send bacon. Thank you, Love, The Woodrow.

I had expected a robust online response—Woodrow, the George Clooney of dogs, with his running commentary on the foibles of humans, was popular. And indeed our friends expressed dismay, concern, love; sent wishes for better health, prayers for speedy recovery, stories of their own pets who'd also had congestive heart failure and lived comfortably, with medication, for several more years. What I hadn't anticipated was real-life help. I knew what people did, I'd done it myself, when a human was sick: sending flowers, bringing food. But for my dog! To my surprise, our apartment became a parade of comfort and assistance. My friend Erin, who didn't have a pet, brought Frosty Paws, canine ice cream—"I was shopping and I thought it seemed like something he'd like to eat," she said. My friend Cathy came with organic chicken that had been intended for her husband's dinner. "He'll get takeout," she said, shrugging. My upstairs neighbor Jamie, when she heard Woodrow wouldn't eat, brought a whole rotisserie roaster. "I thought maybe he just wanted something different," she said. "You know how they work you like that." She looked at Woodrow sleeping and squeezed my arm. "Oh, it's so hard," she said and fled upstairs.

Along with my gratitude and amazement, I was uncomfortable. I'd never learned to ask for help. I hated it. It was something else I'd inherited from my parents, a companion to that stubbornness gene. You didn't burden other people with your problems; you handled them yourself. Once I'd sprained my wrist turning over my Minnesota garden with a spade instead of borrowing my neighbor's Rototiller. As a teenager, when my dad had his own heart issues and my mom went to law school, then worked as an attorney to support the family, I'd cared for my younger siblings: shopping, cleaning, cooking the meals after school, feeding and bathing my much-younger brother and reading him books before bed. It never occurred to me to reach out for help. Why would I? Admitting you needed it was a sign of weakness.

Now, lying on the rug with Woodrow, I tried not to think of the weeks and months ahead. How I'd get him up and down the stairs. How to get him to the Angell if I had to, without Jim to lift Woodrow into my high-clearance Jeep. How I'd work, leaving the house to teach and attend book events and readings. Woodrow's sitter Alyson had come to visit us, and we both teared up watching Woodrow sleep. "I have to ask you," I said, "what's your caretaking limit? It's not easy to take him out, and he's having a hard time eating . . ."

Alyson shook her head. "There's no limit," she said. "I'm happy to do anything Woodrow needs."

That would have to do. We had Alyson and food delivery, and I'd just figure the rest out. I'd already canceled my events for the next couple of weeks, until Woodrow's condition stabilized . . . or didn't. There was one more thing I needed to do now, something I'd never done before.

I positioned my head against Woodrow's ribs, took out my iPhone, and hit record.

"Hi, everybody," I said. "So tonight's the paperback launch for my third novel, *The Lost Family*, and I'm supposed to be at the enchanted bookstore An Unlikely Story in Plainville, Massachusetts, with mega-superstar Queen Jane Green." Jane was a *New York Times* bestseller multiple times over; she was so successful and elegant, with her velvet British voice and gorgeous pink hair, that I would have had to hate her if she weren't also so human and lovely, the kind of woman who had a giant bangle full of tequila for her tour events and who'd invited me into her kitchen, into her backyard to feed her chickens; our friendship was one of my safe places in the world. We'd planned this evening, our joint appearance, for months, shopping long-distance, sending each other fitting-room selfies. Jane would wear a gold caftan and I a silver disco-ball dress; we had matching false eyelashes. The bookstore's events manager, Kym Havens, and her chef husband had created a banquet for us and the attending readers of food based on my and Jane's novels. It was a big deal, a launch; the paperback especially was a book's second and final lease on life, and it could make or break sales. Tonight was going to be a hell of a party, and I was defaulting. Jane would be carrying the evening solo. Of course you must stay with Woodrow, darling, she'd texted. I've got you.

"Jane's new hardcover, *The Friends We Keep*, launches tonight," I said to the phone, "and I was so looking forward to celebrating with you all. The only way I'd miss the launch for my third baby is that my first baby is sick," and I panned the camera to show Woodrow sleeping behind me. "Woodrow, my fourteen-year-old Lab, went into heart failure this week. He's doing better now, thanks in large part to your amazing support. But I can't leave him right now, so celebrate Queen Jane for me, okay? And I'll see you a little farther down the road."

I signed off, put the phone down. "Pretty good, huh, Kooks?" I said. "Our first-ever IGTV appearance." Woodrow didn't move. I picked up one of his paws, held it in my hand. Its pads were worn smooth as stones from all his years of running and walking; he'd started slipping on my wooden floors this year, and my apartment was as full of rugs as a souk. His paw also smelled like corn chips, and it was warm. I could feel Woodrow's pulse in it. I put it against my face and remembered an afternoon when he was ten weeks old and I'd picked him up and laid him on my chest for a nap on the couch. I'd been struck with wonder that for the first time, I was responsible for a creature with a heart. Then it had beat like a fierce little jackhammer. Now it thudded slowly, heavily, against my cheek.

The next morning I awoke in the same position, my back and neck stiff. My parents had complained when, as a little girl, I'd wanted them to play board games with me on the floor. Now I understood. "It's no fun to get old, is it, Kooks," I said. "But think of the alternative!" Woodrow stirred, exhaling a gust of low-tide breath in my face, but otherwise didn't move.

The doorbell rang. I wasn't expecting anyone, and I hoped it wasn't a friend dropping by unannounced. I needed a shower and to change the clothes I'd slept in—and to try and feed Woodrow, give him his meds, get him outside. The doorbell shrilled again. "Okay, okay, I'm coming," I said.

I jogged down the building's steps into the foyer, praying for the UPS man or our postal carrier Jeff with a package—

they'd seen me in all manner of disarray, poor guys. Instead, I was horrified to see, waving at me through the glass door, Kym Havens—the bookstore events manager I'd stood up for my launch the night before. She smiled, holding up an armful of paper bags. Tall purple flowers arced gracefully from one of them.

"Oh my God," I said, opening the door. "What are you doing here?" If delivery people, neighbors, and some of my friends had seen me au naturel, I had never, and I mean never, encountered a bookstore employee without my game face on. For every event, I went full-court press: dressed in outfits to match my book covers (always red), slathered on the Lady Gaga makeup, wanded or put up my hair. I knew some writers didn't dress up—they were writers, after all, not performers—but for me it was more than the chance to get out of the house and into leather pants. It was a sign of respect for my hosts, bookstore staff, and readers. If they were going to give up their precious time not only to read my books but to come hear me talk about them, I was going to give them a show.

Now here was Kym, a human sunflower with her curly blond hair and cheerful face, and I was in the sagging yoga capris I'd worn for three days and my Mister Brisket MeatMobile T-shirt. I couldn't remember the last time I'd bathed. I tried not to breathe on Kym, as I hadn't brushed my teeth the night before, either.

"Hi, sweetie!" she said. "I saw your IGTV post last night

and I just felt so bad for you!" See, I thought, this was what happened when you admitted weakness; people pitied you. "I wanted to bring you some goodies," Kym added, "and meet Mr. Woodrow. How is he?"

"Sleeping," I said. "That's what he does most of the time right now. Please, come on up, although I warn you the place is a bit messy."

"Oh, are you sure?" Kym said. "I don't want to disturb him. Or you."

"No, it's fine," I said, and it was: Plainville, where Kym's bookstore was located, was an hour south of Boston, and the least I could do after she'd driven all this way was invite her in. The apartment was blanketed in drop cloths like the lair of a psychotic painter, but sans further Poopsplosion, it was fairly clean.

"He'll be happy to see you," I said. "He might not be too demonstrative, but he'll know you're there."

"I'll just give him a kiss and tiptoe away," said Kym as she followed me upstairs.

I opened the apartment door, and to my astonishment, not only was Woodrow awake, he was sitting up and smiling. His tail began to thump when he saw Kym.

"Oh, there he is," she cried. "Look how handsome! No, don't get up, sweet boy," she said, because Woodrow was trying to struggle to his feet.

"I can't believe it," I said. "He hasn't gotten up on his own all week."

"I'm so honored," said Kym, setting down her bags and sitting on the floor. I raced over to help Woodrow, to lift him using his harness, but he was already walking stiffly over to Kym, kicking out his rear right leg. "Oh my goodness," she said, laughing, as he licked her face.

"Well," I said. "He always did know a beautiful lady when he sees one." I was amazed by Woodrow's Lazarus-like transformation. All week, as we'd lain on the rug, I'd thought uneasily of that promise I'd made to myself, that I'd made him: *If the nose and tail no longer work* . . . I'd felt his spirit slipping away from me a bit more each day, like a little boat bobbing out toward the horizon. One morning I'd wake up, and it'd be gone. All week, secretly, I'd been wondering: Was this it? Was it time to let go? Now Woodrow stomped all over Kym's lap, her legs, trying to get to the grocery bags she'd brought. He stuck his snout all the way in the nearest one.

"Oh, Woodrow, no," I said. "I'm sorry!"

"Don't be," Kym said, laughing. "He knows there's something in here for him."

She handed me a Tupperware container. "Bacon," she said. "I know from his Instagram that he loves it."

"He does," I said. I opened the container and tossed him a piece, which he caught in midair. "I'll be damned," I said. "And what other magic is in those bags?"

"It's food from last night," Kym said. "I thought since you couldn't come to the launch, the launch could come to you. There's brisket, latkes with crème fraîche and beet dip, profiteroles . . ." She was listing the food that my chef character, Peter, featured in his restaurant in my book. "And Masha's chocolate torte," she finished, "which of course was a big hit. We didn't light the cherries flambé, because fire code. But I brought you some anyway."

"I seriously cannot believe you did all this," I said. "To drive all the way up here to bring me food you made for the launch I stood you up for . . ."

"Shush," said Kym. "For the best possible cause," and she gave Woodrow another strip of bacon.

"And what are those beautiful flowers?" I asked of the long slender stems.

"Irises," said Kym. "From my garden. I just cut them this morning. . . . Oh, sweetie! Don't cry!"

But I couldn't help it. I shook my head and tried to excuse myself, blew my nose on some napkins Kym had brought and accepted her strong hug. When I was done, we sat on the floor with Woodrow and unpacked the food, picnicked on the brisket and latkes as though it were Passover. Which, in a way, it was. Sometimes, it seems, when you let people know what you're going through, help arrives when you're least expecting it, bringing you what you didn't know you needed, in forms above and beyond what you've ever imagined.

Devin from Heaven

After Jim goes back to Minnesota, I face a real challenge: getting Woodrow up the building's stairs by myself. Getting Woodrow down is a cautious process but doable, as long as we take it slowly, with me gripping his rear harness handle and leash, so he doesn't overbalance and topple us over. But he's still not strong enough to get up by himself, so at first Jim picks him up and carries him. We make a game of it: "Get ready for Flying W!" we cry in the building lobby, as Jim hefts Woodrow like an oversize black lamb. "Here comes Flying W! Flying W—wheeeeee!" Jim jogs with Woodrow up the steps as Woodrow looks back at me, his droll expression saying: *You humans invent the MOST fucked-up ways of having fun.* But it also says: *Well, this isn't so bad. Why haven't you been carrying me up the stairs my whole life?*

To my mortification and concern, though, I can't do Flying W on my own. At five two and slender, I can serve a mean ace, throw a half hour of uppercuts, run a daily 5K—but I don't have the upper-body strength to dead-lift my eighty-five-pound dog. I try but fail to scoop him into my arms the way Jim does, and when I lift Woodrow by the harness handles—his legs dangling, the straps pressing into his stomach in a way that looks wretchedly uncomfortable—he struggles so much that he unbalances us both. It isn't safe. I am so angry with myself. Why did I spend all those years at the gym doing cardio? Why didn't I ever anticipate that someday I might have to carry my heavy Lab? My friend and neighbor Jacqulene could do it; she's a weight lifter, and whenever her own black Lab Rizzo refuses to get up and walk home, she just slings him over her shoulder and hauls him there, all ninety pounds of him. Jacqulene would be happy to help me with Woodrow—but I can't ask her to come twice a day, morning and evening. She has a job.

In the week before Jim leaves, we spend hours researching options: constructing a ramp on the building's stairs, then wheeling Woodrow up in a cart? There are such things, I discover: a whole industry devoted to dogs who can't walk. There are legit canine strollers, which I've seen in the hands of pet parents whose charges are lame or otherwise incapacitated, the dogs whizzing along with their ears back and tongues flying. These prams, like the ones for children, are elaborate. They have mesh sides for breathability, beverage holders, dune-buggy wheels for navigating city curbs, tailgates that fold down. But they're not built for big dogs, and the reviewers caution against using them for animals that weigh as much as Woodrow. He'll fall out.

"Maybe you could use a sled," my friend Sara suggests.

"But there are still stairs, Sara," her husband Nunnally says. "How would the sled get up the stairs?"

"It would SLIDE up, Nunnally," Sara says. "OBVI. DUH."

"I wish we could rig up a dumbwaiter for him," Jim says. "Then you could winch him right up over the front door into the apartment."

Whatever the talk of dog elevators, carts, and Flexible Flyers, the fact remains: the only way to get Woodrow up the stairs is muscle. "I don't know how you're going to do this," Jim says the night before he leaves, watching me try to hoist Woodrow using his harness handles.

I want to punch Jim. This is precisely why I hate the long-distance relationship—in addition to other factors: it often leaves me on my own to do the not only difficult but sometimes impossible. I summon all my pioneer-ancestor cheer: "I'll figure it out," I say. I leave the codicil unspoken: I'll have to. I have no choice.

The morning after Jim leaves, I get Woodrow downstairs and outside without mishap: "Slow, Kooks," I say as we lurch down each step. "Slow slow slow. Good boy. I've got you." We're both panting by the time we reach the bench. It's a hot, humid morning, one of those summer days when even if you've taken a shower—which I haven't—you don't feel like you have because you're sweaty again seconds later. I pour water from Woodrow's Gulpy into a Tupperware container, which he takes a few laps from and then upsets in the dirt, per usual. I sigh. It has been a rough morning. Woodrow didn't sleep much. Neither did I. In the kitchen, he ate three bites of mac and cheese and then turned his head, even when I sat on the floor to hand-feed him; finally, in desperation, I forced his meds down his slippery throat. Then the laborious journey to the bench. Now I am hot, exhausted again, sticky, stinky, and covered in flecks of homemade dog food. And I still have no idea how I'll get Woodrow back up the stairs.

"God help me," I say. "God help us both, right, Kooks?" Woodrow puts his snout in the dirt. I shut my eyes. I breathe in and out, longer on the exhale, as Sara has taught me. I listen to cicadas in the trees, music from cars passing on Commonwealth. I feel perspiration rolling down my rib cage and neck. I smell cut grass the city has recently mown on the Mall and exhaust from the traffic. I hear cardinals calling and the soft *whump* as Woodrow flops over onto his side. Years ago, when I was involved with a codependency recovery group, I learned that to say gratitudes for even the most trying moments is a way of saying, *At least I'm alive*. That a simple *Thank you* sent heavenward is the most perfect prayer. It's unbelievably annoying advice, but it works. Thank you, I think. Also help. Thank you.

When I open my eyes I reach in the backpack for more water and my fingers touch a business card I don't remember receiving. Did Jim put it in there, when he took Woodrow out before he left? BIG DOG, LITTLE DOG, the card says, next to a cartoon canine pack. DOG WALKING AND SERVICES OF ALL KINDS. I play with the card, worrying its corners. I still dislike asking for help. I don't know if I can afford it, paying somebody to come for Woodrow twice a day. Also, I hate talking on the phone. I text like a tween, but I use the phone for its intended purpose only in emergencies.

I call the number on the card. "Hello?" a man says.

"I have a sort of weird question," I say. "Do you ever carry dogs up the stairs?"

Half an hour later a dark-haired young man ambles toward us under the trees, accompanied by the real-life version of the cartoon pack on the card. Dogs of all shapes and sizes, from dachshund to beagle to shaggy mutt, strain on a tangle of leashes, while a beautiful Aslan-like golden retriever, off-leash, trots alongside the man. "This is Tuck," says the man when he reaches us, "and this is the Wacky Pack. I'm Devin." He attaches the Wacky Pack's leashes to the bench and sits cross-legged on the grass next to Woodrow, who perks up. "This must be Woodrow," Devin says. "What's going on, buddy? You got arthritis in those back legs?"

I wonder how Devin knows this, since Woodrow is still lying down, although it's a common problem in old Labs. "He does, and he's got congestive heart failure, too," I say. "He's doing better now, but it's hard on him, this heat."

"Well, sure," says Devin. "Nobody likes this weather, especially when they reach such a distinguished age." Woodrow props his snout on Devin's knee, and Devin starts combing his hands backward through Woodrow's fur, sifting out the hot downy undercoat, which rolls away in tumbleweeds down the Mall. "They like that," Devin explains, "it relaxes them," and indeed Woodrow heaves a sigh, his eyes closing. The Wacky Pack sniffs Woodrow curiously; Tuck the Golden stands guard, ready to show teeth if anyone gets too fresh.

In the next few weeks, I will learn that Devin is from Iowa, where his family has a farm. That his girlfriend Lucy is a contract RN, and they go wherever Lucy's work takes her. That Devin was in the service for a time, having joined the army out of high school. Devin from Heaven, the dog moms on the block call him, and not just because he shows up every morning and evening to whisk Woodrow up the stairs. He is admittedly easy on the eyes. But what I remember most about Devin is his low soothing voice, not what he says but the tone of it, murmuring about everything and nothing and requiring no response as his big square hands comb restlessly, gently, through Woodrow's fur. And how completely, for those minutes, I relax.

After that few weeks, Lucy's job ends, and she and Devin and Tuck are on the move again. The Wacky Pack has to find a new walker as they disappear, back to Iowa or maybe California or who knows where. I never find out, although sometimes I wonder, the same way I wonder whether Devin's affinity for animals, his way of knowing what pains or helps them on any given day, is the result of somebody who has himself been hurt by humans. I wonder over the fact of Devin's time in Boston lasting almost exactly as long as it takes for Woodrow to improve enough to start climbing the stairs on his own.

But I don't know any of that on this hot June morning. I know only that I sent that prayer heavenward and it was granted, in the form of this young man. Who's standing now, brushing the grass from his shorts. "You ready to go in, buddy?"

I start to grab Woodrow's harness, then force myself to step back. "We're ready," I say. "Thank you. So, have you ever played a game called the Flying W?"

July

YOU ARE NOT INVISIBLE

One of the great things about owning a dog is that you never wake up alone. I've been blessed with lovely partners, and our times have come and gone—and through them all, Andy, the guy I dated after Andy, and Jim, Woodrow remained. And slept on the bed. For thirteen years, whether we had human company or not, I started every morning with Woodrow looming over me—wearing what I called his Lincoln Face, not just because his head was Mount Rushmore size from that angle but because of his somber expression. *Something is amiss. Something is very wrong. The dog is starving.* If I didn't move quickly enough to suit him, waves of hot damp dog morning breath washed over me. We'd turn to lie sideways across the bed, facing the big window overlooking Commonwealth Avenue, and I'd raise the shade so Woodrow could survey his domain, the Mall, and all the humans and canines strolling thereto. His eyes filled with light as he watched them. "Good morning, Woodrow," I said. "I am awake, and you are awake, and that makes it a good day."

The year Woodrow turned thirteen, this routine changed because he could no longer make the stairs to my sleeping loft, which were very narrow and steep, like the ones to Anne Frank's famous Secret Annex. Rather than torment him by forcing him up, I got him an orthopedic bed I set at the foot of the stairs and climbed them myself, sleeping alone for the first time in over a decade. I mourned that night, quietly. But when I came downstairs the next day, Woodrow was awake and waiting for me. His tail thumped, his eyes shining just as they had in the loft. *Good morning, Mommoo. I am awake, and you are awake, and it is a good day.*

This July, after Jim went back to Minnesota, our routine shifted yet again. Woodrow had improved considerably. His heartbeat was steady, his appetite back, his breathing regular. As Dr. Zarin had predicted, it had taken him about two weeks to adjust to his meds. But Woodrow's ability to move around by himself was compromised, so in order to make his needs known, he had developed the yark. The yark was a tiny little baby bark that sounded as though it were being forced through a wheezy accordion—

yark!
yark!
yark!

—all Woodrow's old vocal cords could muster. But though it was small, the yark was mighty. It roused me from a sound sleep. It penetrated walls, floors, and doors. It made me do whatever Woodrow wanted, which was one of six things:

1. Bring me food!
2. Please take me out!
3. Move me from place to place!
4. I require water!
5. I want to play, roll my ball to me!
6. Didn't you hear me, lazy woman? I am starving!

A yark in the night could also mean—

7. Warning! Poopsplosion is imminent!

. . . so I had quickly learned to pay attention. Now my response was Pavlovian. Woodrow yarked, and I jumped.

Our new morning routine revolved around the yark. *Yark!* I snapped awake and went downstairs. Woodrow thumped his tail and twinkled his bottom teeth at me. He had lost a few more, and the survivors were tilted like Stonehenge. *Yark! Good morning, Mommoo!* "Good morning, Woodrow," I said. "I am awake, and you are awake, and it's a good day." I sat next to him to rub his bony back and hindquarters— he'd lost a lot of muscle mass from lack of exercise, but sometimes the massaging helped him walk. *Yark!* "What's that? You're hungry?" *Yark! That is a stupid question, Mommoo.* "Okay, Kooks. I hear you." I helped him stand with the aid of his harness—if he was feeling good, Woodrow pushed himself up—and we went into the kitchen, where I prepared the chicken and rice he spattered all over the walls like a canine lawn sprinkler. I made my coffee and packed our backpack and we went outside, making our slow way down the steps, across Commonwealth, and along the Mall to the bench. There I helped Woodrow settle in his spot, gave him water, took out my own work, and sat.

And we sat and sat. And sat.

Boston is a tidal city, its population ebbing and flowing with the seasons. In summer it empties out, the residents migrating to the Cape, to the islands, to Berkshires retreats. In the fall they return, along with a tsunami of students—September 1 is the worst for parking, because of all the U-Hauls and moving trucks. For most of the year I enjoyed the company of my dog-mom friends: Sarah with Harriet, the wheaten terrier who always had a rose on her collar. Beautiful Jacqulene and her black Lab Rizzo. Mary and the "little treat whore" Lucy, who loved her Milk-Bones. Monique and goldendoodle Cashew, who nosed me in places and ways that would have required a human to buy me a drink first. But by Independence Day, everyone was gone. They walked off dragging their dogs and calling cheerily, "See you in a few weeks!" Woodrow and I were on our own.

I sat on the bench with Woodrow, becoming aware of a familiar feeling of having been left behind. It was not a good one. I'd forgotten about it, because in previous years I'd been with Jim, or traveling, or on book tour, in Minnesota at my family house, at the beach. But now, stranded under the big trees, as I looked up and down the Mall while Woodrow reclined in the dirt, that bad old feeling came back to me like a language I'd learned a long time ago in a country I didn't like. It was the feeling of being alone and invisible. I hadn't felt it this strongly—or at all—since the last summer I was on my own, two decades before. In the last century, a different millennium, even. The summer I got divorced.

My husband hadn't wanted to get divorced; it was my idea. Sean was British, a lovely exuberant guy who was a cross between Indiana Jones—he had traveled the world by the time he was nineteen—and Steve Irwin, the late Crocodile Hunter, who, with his floppy honey-colored hair and great, often misplaced enthusiasm, Sean very much resembled. In later years, every time I saw Irwin exclaim "Cor, there's a real beauty!" about a rattlesnake or baby gator he was prodding with a stick, and the reptile snapped back in vicious self-defense, I'd think: Yup, there's Sean.

I was obsessed with *My Fair Lady* when I was a kid, and it was in the spot where Professor Henry Higgins first encounters Eliza Doolittle, in London's Covent Garden, that I met Sean. I was on my junior year abroad, guzzling snakebite and blacks as quickly as only a person liberated from her country's drinking age could, and Sean was out with his mates. I don't recall his opening line—something involving knickers—but I apparently gave him my phone number, which he put to good use the next morning. By the following evening I was again at Covent Garden, this time doing my first tequila shots. One thing led to another, Jose Cuervo to nightclub to bed to courtship to travel to relationship conducted via letter in air mail envelopes and expensive phone calls to engagement, and the next thing I knew, at an age when all of my college friends were getting entry-level jobs and moving to Brooklyn and Hoboken, I was married.

We married for love, which is not a bad reason. But we had failed to take into consideration issues such as what we wanted our lives to be like, or our value sets, or where we wanted to live. The week before the wedding, we discovered Sean thought we'd be residing in England, whereas I didn't want to leave the States. Having agreed on the US for a year, we tried to build a home. Sean's exuberance, a lovely characteristic in general, wasn't well suited to domesticity or steady employment; he was like Jack in *Jack and the Beanstalk*, leaving the house in the morning a debt collector and returning that afternoon to announce, "Bad news, sausage, I was made redundant—but good news, I'm now selling personal massagers!" Nor was his bounding energy a good match for a wife who wanted to be a writer.

"What you doing, then?" he'd ask, popping his head into my study, which was also our bedroom. "Cor, you're not writing anything—you're just looking at the wall!" No matter how many times I tried to explain that gazing into space was part of writing, Sean wasn't buying it. "How long until you'll be done, then?" he'd demand. "Right, sausage, I'll be back in an hour and we'll go play some tennis!"

In the end, this was what broke us up: I needed to be a writer, and Sean needed other things. A family, for one. His sisters made beautiful babies, multitudes of them, rosy-cheeked and flaxen-haired like children in a fairy tale. "I don't want to be an old dad," he said plaintively in our endless conversations about this. "How long's writing a book going to take you, then?" I explained, as I had before, that there was no mathematical formula for writing and publishing a novel—alas. One hot day right before the turn of the millennium, we had this discussion again—we were naked on my bed, having just indulged in an afternoon delight; love was not the problem with us. I reiterated that I had to write novels—at least two—before I had children, or I'd never do it, and then I'd end up pinched and bitter. "All I ever wanted was to be a writer," I said. Sean sprang up and dressed. "All right," he said. "Have a nice life," and he was out the door.

I expected him to come back. After all of our arguments, he always came back. I went to work at my desk, anticipating that in a few hours he'd be bouncing up and down outside my window as if he were on a pogo stick, yelling, "Let me in, silly sausage! Let's kiss and make up!" But he didn't. The window remained empty, and we got divorced, and a few years later I saw him on Facebook holding a predictably beautiful baby. I was happy for him then. But right after he disappeared, all I knew was that I was confused, like a puppy waiting for its playmate to come back, and sad, and also a little relieved. What I hadn't expected was to become invisible.

I mean this literally. It was the summer of 2000. I wasn't teaching. All my neighbors were gone, my friends, too. It was the time of life, early thirties, when everyone got married; my peers were off planning weddings or acclimating to new in-laws, buying houses, second houses, wine cellars. I was newly single, the odd girl out in the mating version of musical chairs. I was working on my first book, about as solitary an endeavor as there can be. I started going to Starbucks every morning so I could hear the barista say, "One venti iced espresso, have a great day!" Once out of school, working for yourself, how did you meet people? I was stumped. I couldn't do it in bars; a woman sitting alone picked up the kind of company I was not looking for. I haunted the Whole Foods at the end of my block, buying ridiculously expensive grapes one day, an outrageously priced bar of soap the next, fearing I was becoming one of those women who goes to the supermarket on Saturday nights for a can of peas. I sat in the Public Garden all day every day with a book, looking up with a hopeful smile each time somebody passed, like a person running a yard sale. As summer wore on, I started contemplating what would happen if I marched into my local pizza joint and announced, "I'll sleep with any guy here."

One steamy gray August afternoon I was taking the T from my neighborhood to Harvard Square to go to a bookstore—maybe there I could strike up a conversation with some like-minded literary people. The platform was nearly empty. The few travelers waiting for the train drooped in the heat. It was the age before iPhones, too, so they read newspapers or books, stared vacantly down the track for the train. A gentleman came up the steps from the street, bespectacled and natty in suit and bow tie. As he passed me, he bumped into me, hard. "Hey!" I said, when he walked on. "Excuse me!" He didn't turn around. "You bumped into me," I called. "Hey!" The gentleman took a spot at the far end of the platform and shook out his *Boston Globe*. It was official. I had become invisible.

In *The Great Gatsby*, narrator Nick Carraway says "I had that familiar conviction that life was beginning over again with the summer." For me, this year, the season was an abyss, like walking down a well-known street and falling into a manhole. I should have been watching; I should have foreseen better and prepared for potential isolation. But how? Since Sean, I had not married again, although there had been a series of long relationships with terrific men whose lifestyles had not matched mine—including Andy, the guy who brought me Woodrow. I didn't know what had happened to Sean beyond that one Facebook glimpse; the next time I looked for him there, he'd disappeared. But I had learned my lesson, I thought: after a decade with an IT guy here, a scientist there, I had chosen, in Jim, a creative. And it was true that Jim, a world-renowned photographer, knew what it meant when he knocked on the door of my study and I made frantic helicopter motions with my hands: *Go away*. It was also true that Jim did go away. A lot. It was part of his job description—pro shooters travel by necessity—and part of his personality. Once, when we were discussing our possible future, Jim said, "How about if I contribute some sperm and then I can come back in my RV and visit our offspring every once in a while?" I threw my coffee mug into the bushes and walked off.

I had broken off our engagement the previous Christmas, eight months before. Jim and I had been together a decade by then, enfianced for almost half that time. The decision to end the betrothal was based on one of the harder lessons of my life: that love doesn't necessarily conquer everything, including what my therapist called "incongruent relationship goals." I had a goal: a live-in partner

I loved, with whom I'd build a life. I wasn't sure—even after repeatedly asking—that Jim knew what his was. "I love the *idea* of that," he always said about marriage. Once more, love was not the issue. Positioning was. It was like another lesson I talked about with my friend Kirsten: in our early thirties, we'd made wish lists of attributes we wanted in our future husbands, magneted them onto our refrigerators, offered them up to the universe. Jim checked every box on my list and then some. I adored that man. I'd found in him qualities I'd always wanted in a mate— humor, intelligence, kindness, physical attraction, curiosity, creativity—and some that were pure icing, like his ability to do accents, our shared love of soundtracks and documentaries, his photographic genius. But I'd forgotten to ask another crucial question: What attributes do you want in the relationship?

Until this summer, I'd remained hopeful: even after we tearfully agreed we weren't in the same place, literally and emotionally, after we'd taken off our rings and nestled them together in a blue velvet box in my fireproof safe in case we changed our minds, Jim and I were . . . connected. We were still each other's person. A fast learner in life, I was much slower in relationships. That stubbornness thing again: I was loath to give up on people I loved.

But as I sat on the bench, Woodrow panting in the dust beside me, I realized that although Jim always boomeranged back, though there was that tantalizing possibility of "maybe someday," what we had between that mirage and this moment was not enough. We still had a long-distance . . . something, secured by phone calls every other day or so and lots of Bitmojis. It was insufficient. It was unsustainable. It had led me to precisely where I never wanted to be and exactly where now I was: here. Without a partner to share life's burdens and joys and waking routines and bench sits, without even a couple of surly teenagers to remind me how terminally uncool I was. Reliant instead upon friends and neighbors with whom there was mutual adoration but who couldn't always be there because their families, of course, came first. Here I was, alone with my dog beneath some big trees. I was once again invisible.

Except.

The key phrase was "with my dog."

The last time I'd spent a summer in Boston on my own, I hadn't had a dog.

I hadn't factored Woodrow into the equation. How could I have forgotten that he was a canine Venus fly trap? Luring passersby in with his elegant crossed paws and big smile, then pinning them there. If all the residents had fled the city, tourists flooded in for the Glorious Fourth; bedecked in flag shirts, flag bandannas, and flag tank tops, carrying flag Koozies, they came from state after state to experience Independence Day in the cradle of the Revolution, only to be pulled in by Woodrow's tractor beam. A farmer and his wife from Illinois, who paused to say "We left our yellow Lab at home" and stayed to talk about the surplus of rain drowning their corn crop. A quartet from Alaska, two couples celebrating their fifty-year friendship. A beautiful Italian woman in white jeans who sat right down in the dirt with Woodrow and said, over and over, "He is so special, this one. I can tell, he has such a special soul," and started to cry, patting his head, until her boyfriend, apologizing profusely and unnecessarily, pulled her away.

There was the young girl who had just left polygamy in Utah and tried nonetheless to interest me in the Book of Mormon; the homeless woman who told me that before her mom's illness and death bankrupted her she'd been a neuroscientist, and could I direct her to the nearest shelter for lunch? (I could.) The City Council candidate who asked for our vote. The Parks Department employee, Charles, who came up to us every morning with his garbage-impaling stick and asked Woodrow, "How you doin', my brother? Staying out of trouble?" He's trying, I said. "Me too, my brother, me too." How's that working out for you? I asked, to which Charles replied, "Not so well, not so well. I keep trying. But not succeeding, thank God." Charles was always trying to stay out of trouble but never quite managing. "Have yourself a blessed day, sister," he'd say to me with a fist bump before walking away.

One evening, just as dusk was falling under the trees, two women walked past. I now waited until the sun was down before taking Woodrow out for the nightly bench sit, since it was cooler then and easier on his heart. He had just settled into the dirt with his Tupperware bowl of water, which he promptly knocked over, and I was opening my iPad when they came up to us, a lady a few years older than me in linen trousers and a gauzy summer top and a younger one in Daisy Dukes, floppy hat, and sandals. They introduced themselves as mother and daughter, living a few blocks away, and the mother exclaimed, "Thank goodness you're here! We didn't see you for a few days and we were so worried that something had . . . happened to him." She gestured to Woodrow.

"We've been coming out later in the day because of the heat," I explained, to which they both said *Ahhhhh*. Yes, the mother said, they'd started walking later in the evenings, too.

The daughter was kneeling with Woodrow, stroking his head and murmuring to him. Woodrow put his snout in her lap and rolled his eyes up in what I privately called his Jesus expression: *Thank you, lady. My Mommoo never feeds or pets me.* Oh FFS, I thought.

"How old is he?" the daughter asked.

"Almost fifteen," I said. "His birthday's in September. I'll have a big party out here for him if he's still here . . . if you want to come."

"We'd love to," the mother said, and the daughter nodded. Woodrow had laid his head down on her tanned thigh and closed his eyes in bliss.

"We'll pray he makes it," the mom said. "We pray for you every day."

"You *do*?" I said.

The daughter nodded. "Yup," she said. "We always pray we'll see you."

"We always look for you," the mother confirmed. "Every time we take a walk, we see you out here with him, so devoted, so patient with him and kind, and it reminds us to practice a little more patience and kindness in our daily lives."

"Wow," I said. I really was stunned. "That's amazing. Thank you for telling me that. But I'm not sure I'm the greatest example. I do get cross with him sometimes—when it's hot, or when it's tough to get him in and out of the building . . ."

"Well, sure," said the lady. "What you're doing is so hard. But you didn't give up, you didn't just put him down when the going got tough. A lot of people would, you know. But here you are, out here with him every day, giving him the gift of time."

I had to swallow a lump. "It's he who gives me the gift," I said. "I'm the lucky one."

"Yes," the woman said, "our animals do that, don't they?"

We said our goodbyes, promising to look for one another in the future, and they strolled off down the Mall, disappearing into the evening shadows beneath the canopy of the big trees. I sat back and looked at Woodrow.

"How about that, Kooks?" I said. He looked off down the conveyor belt of the path that would bring him more visitors, smiling and panting. *I already knew that, Mommoo.* It was quite possible that Woodrow did indeed already know something I had not: with a dog, you are always visible. And you are never really invisible at all: all you have to do to be part of somebody's daily life, that fabric of a community, is show up at the same place every day, same time, and be present. Here I am again, I had started the evening thinking, and I'd been right without knowing it. *I am here.*

JuJo

The first time I meet Casey to audition her as Woodrow's pet sitter, I don't think she'll be able to handle my physically demanding dog. Hauling him around. Lifting him to his feet. Getting him up and down the stairs. Casey is a tiny thing, a slip of a girl, coming only up to my shoulder—and I'm five two—and slender as a fingernail moon. She has a luster of dark curls, a bouclé jacket, a scarf tied around her neck like a French lady, and, most damningly, kitten heels. "Are you sure you can do this?" I ask, as she grips Woodrow's harness on the building landing. I believe Woodrow outweighs her by ten pounds.

"Uh-huh," she says.

"Really?" I ask.

"Sure," she says.

She eases Woodrow down the stairs without a hitch, heels clacking. Her balance is better than mine, her posture queenlike. She doesn't grab for the banister or say "Slow, slow slow" in a warning voice. I follow her and Woodrow outside.

"What's his routine?" she asks, once we're standing on the grass of the Mall.

"He'll do his sniffs," I say, "and then probably his peeps, and then he'll take you to the bench. I told you about the bench, right?"

"I believe you mentioned it."

"Yes, well, you should schedule an extra half an hour for the bench," I say. "I mean, if your work schedule permits it. I always allow ten minutes to get Woodrow inside, another ten for outside, and at least a half hour on the bench."

"Okay," Casey says, holding on to Woodrow as he performs exactly the sequence I just described, then starts pulling determinedly toward his bench. *Come on, LADY. I will show you.* "I guess this is it?" Casey says, as Woodrow WHUMPS down in his spot.

"This is it," I say. "Welcome to the bench." I sit. She sits. I take Woodrow's water out of his backpack, pour it in his Tupperware; he laps at it, spills the rest into the dirt. "There's extra water in here," I add.

"I can see why," she says. "That was pretty messy, Woodrow." She leans over, scratching Woodrow's head with her prettily manicured nails. He slits his eyes in bliss and pants happily.

"Also," I say, "you might want to budget time for the Woodrow effect."

"What's that?"

"You'll see," I say.

"That sounds mysterious," says Casey with a little laugh.

"It is," I agree.

I sip coffee from my traveler. Casey pets Woodrow and tucks wind-blown curls behind her ears before they can get stuck in her lipstick. Sure enough, after about five minutes of people strolling past and smiling, a couple stops. They're older, in their late seventies or early eighties, she with short curls and floral pants, he in a blue plaid flannel shirt and feed cap of the sort you don't see much around downtown Boston but which are ubiquitous in my mom's rural Minnesota hometown. Farmers, I guess, and tourists for sure. "Oh, what a darling," says the woman. "May we say hi?"

"He'd love that," I say, and the couple stoops and murmurs to Woodrow. The man's hand is as big and weathered as a baseball mitt, the fingers gnarled and knobby in a way you also never see in cities.

"I'm guessing this guy's not a youngster," says the man, massaging Woodrow's ears in a way that makes Woodrow close his eyes in rapture.

"He's almost fifteen," I say.

"A centenarian!" the man says, straightening with a grimace. "I know how you feel, old buddy. He got arthritis?"

"Now, Jonas, maybe she doesn't want to talk about that," says the woman.

"No, it's fine," I say. "He's got arthritis and heart failure. Or he did, earlier this summer. But medication and bone broth brought him back."

"Did you say bone broth?" she asks.

"I did," I say. "My friend Sara made it for us."

"That's a good friend," she says. "Bone broth's not easy to make."

"She is," I agree.

"That's what we sold on our farm," she says. "Bone broth. That was our specialty. We were dairy farmers in central Pennsylvania before we retired, just last year. Cattle first, then we got into the broth."

"Takes a whole carcass just to make a few quarts," says the man. "And takes a whole week to boil down. We were cooking bones twenty-four/seven."

"That's a lot of bones," I say, looking over at Casey. She seems unfazed, stroking Woodrow's head.

"Sure is," says the man. "Luckily, we had a ready bone supply."

"Oh, Jonas," says the woman. "They don't want to hear about that."

"We shipped that broth all over the country," he says. "From our farm. JuJo Acres. That's us," and he points to Judy and then to himself with a finger knotted as a stick. "Judy and Jonas. JuJo."

"I wish we were still doing it," Judy says. "I'd send you some for Mister, here—what's his name?"

"Woodrow," I say. Nobody ever guesses where Woodrow's name comes from—he's named after a Texas Ranger in Larry McMurtry's Pulitzer-winning novel *Lonesome Dove*. But I can tell roughly how old a person is by the response: they either exclaim "Woody!" (born post-1945) or "Woodrow Wilson, eh? Like the president" (pre–World War II).

"Woodrow Wilson, eh?" says Jonas. "Like the president."

"Yessir," I say. "Just like that."

Judy beams down at Woodrow. "If we still had our bone broth farm," she tells him, "I'd ship you a quart a week, Mr. President. It'd cure what ails you. It brought Jonas back to life, you know."

"It did?" I say. "How so—if you don't mind my asking?"

"Oh now, Judy," says Jonas. "They don't want to hear about that."

"I kind of do, actually," I say.

Judy sits on the bench, and Jonas sits next to her and puts his arm around her. "We're here on our fifty-fifth wedding anniversary," she says. "I always wanted to see Boston, so here we are."

"Fifty-five!" I say. "Congratulations."

"You know how we made it this far?" she says.

"Poetry," says Jonas. He leans past Judy and winks. "I write her poems."

"Bone broth," says Judy, ignoring him. "If it weren't for that, we wouldn't be here. Because he almost didn't make it."

"What happened?" I ask. Casey is still scratching Woodrow's head, her long nails describing patterns in the shiny fur. But I think she's listening.

"Well, he had a brain aneurysm while I was out of the house, food shopping, and I came home, and he was lying in the bedroom cold as a stone," Judy says. "He was turning blue already."

"Oh my goodness," I say.

"I called nine-one-one, of course, and while I was waiting I gave him some of our broth. Spooned it down his throat. And do you know it kept him alive until the medics got there?"

"No," I said.

"Yes," says Judy. "Our broth brought him back to life."

"Wow," I say, "that's some advertising."

"You better believe it," Jonas says. "We had that on all our labels years after that. Say, would you young ladies like to hear a poem?"

"Oh, Jonas," says Judy. But I say sure and Casey says sure, so

Jonas stands, opens the satchel he's carrying, takes out a note-book, and reads . . .

To My Wife, Judy
I loved to hear your sleepy voice
This morning on the phone.
I must confess to missin' you
When was last night alone.
I love the freedom that you have
About doin' your own thing.
With Sue or Carol, Lois or Jean,
And all the joys it brings.
The trips and walks, yoga and shoppin'
that so much to you mean.
The conversations, seminars,
You've really got the scene.
When you've done your roamin'
And come back home again,
To dance and laugh and work with me,
Life on our farm's a whirl.
The love we share, the faith and prayer,
I'm glad that you're my girl

"That was lovely," I say.

"Yes," says Casey, "thank you so much."

Jonas puts the notebook back in his satchel and takes Judy's hand. "Nice talking to you, ladies," he says. "But we'd better go.

I've got a hot date." He touches the brim of his hat and off they walk, down the Mall.

Casey is still petting Woodrow, looking after them. "Wow," she says.

I nod. "Yep."

"That's the Woodrow effect?"

"That's it."

"I can definitely budget time for that," she says. She helps Woodrow stand up from his spot, lifting him as easily as Jonas lifted Judy's hand to his lips. She's going to do just fine.

August

HAVE THE BEST DAY EVER

My three favorite sounds in the world: my mom playing Rachmaninoff, Jim's robust laugh, and the giant SPLOOSHO! Woodrow made jumping into any body of water. Like most Labs, bred to retrieve dead birds from waterways, Woodrow loved to swim. If there was water nearby, he had to be in it or he'd cry—the only time he ever made that sound. Whenever we were on the road together, I sought rest stops where he could swim; that dog had been in the Mississippi, Arkansas, and Platte Rivers; Lakes Erie and Superior; a glacial lake near Helena, Montana; a horse pond near an Ohio establishment called Grandpa's Cheese Barn. In Boston, he cruised in circles in the Public Garden fountains like a Zamboni, eating twigs and leaves while the tourists took photos. One of my earlier dog-mom fails involved taking adolescent Woodrow to the Charles River and releasing him into it, believing like a fool he'd come back. Woodrow ignored the ball I'd thrown, having spotted a raft of ducks. He arrowed toward them, and the ducks let him get within inches—then flew off, farther into the river, where they alighted and waited. When Woodrow got close, they did it again. As he reached the central current that would sweep him out to the Atlantic, I raced along the bank, screaming for him to come back and attracting a crowd. We were on the verge of calling the Boston Fire Department to come retrieve my retriever when Woodrow, obeying some mysterious instinct of his own, decided he'd had enough and returned. *What?* he seemed to say, dripping on land as everyone clapped and cheered. *What are you humans making a fuss about now? I just went for a little swim.*

I thought about these watery adventures often now, in August, when it was so hot. The forecast for Boston's late summer is "soup": the temperatures soaring into the triple digits, the humidity dense. The bricks and pavement of the city retained the heat of the day, so even at night Woodrow's paws left prints in the tar. Our one air conditioner and two dehumidifiers were valiant but no match for the weather, and Woodrow's gagging started up again. "This happens with his condition," Dr. Zarin said when I called the Angell. "Just try to keep him as cool as you can." I applied ice cubes to Woodrow's armpits and belly, and Sara came over with box fans we set up next to his bed. That helped. But still, my old boy's breathing was increasingly labored, and every day as we limped out to the bench to sit in the shade of the big trees, I wished I could find him some water. Although the Charles was four blocks away, it might as well have been in Russia.

One day as we made our way back into our building, Woodrow stopping several times with his head down to catch his breath, we ran into John, our maintenance man. John was a Shakespearean actor in his other life and looked a little like Ben Kingsley with a leaf blower. When he saw us he put down his buckets and equipment to say hi to Woodrow. Woodrow docked, lowering his head and tucking it between John's knees. "How you doing, my friend," said John, rubbing Woodrow's ears. Woodrow wagged. "My good old friend," said John, and he looked at me and put his hand on his heart. "It's so hard on them, this heat," he said. "It's too bad we can't find him a pool."

"Yes," I said. "Isn't it?" A lightbulb went off in my head.

When we got inside, I placed an online order, and the next day a box arrived, containing a blue plastic accordion that when opened became a wading pool.

John brought the hose up from our building's scary basement, and we set the pool on the front walkway to fill it. Woodrow sniffed the water, lapped at it, then climbed in and lay down. He set his snout on the edge and promptly dozed off. I brought my work out and sat next to the pool, propping my feet on Woodrow's soaked rump. People passed and smiled. At one point our neighbor Jamie—a building trustee like me—came out, and I thought she might be about to warn me about getting a ticket. Our neighborhood, the historic Back Bay, has very strict rules about what can and cannot go outside buildings, and

Woodrow's blue plastic Amazon pool definitely did not fit the code. Instead, Jamie set a lawn chair and some magazines down next to me and crept away.

Much of August passed this way: Woodrow napped in the water like a hippo, I worked with my feet on his back. Sometimes I set my iPad down and watched Woodrow sleep and thought about those swims when he was younger, how he'd leaped for hours from a rocky cliff into a Minnesota quarry or picked up the lawn sprinkler and chased Jim and me around the yard with it. I thought about my mom's life, too, or rather the end of it, how she went from shopping excursions to sitting in the parking lot at the beach because she was too weak to get out of the car, from sunning on her front walkway with her coffee and the *Palm Beach Post* to watching TV in her bedroom to finally just her bed. Her existence had dwindled like that small white square on old TVs, shrinking until it winked out altogether. Woodrow might wallow, but he would never swim again.

One morning an SUV pulled up, and my friend Kate, silver-haired and elegant in batik shift and aviators, called from the driver's seat, "Anyone here want to go to Westport?"

Woodrow lifted his chin. We both stared at her. "Are you sure?" I said. "It'll be a lot of work."

"It will," she agreed, grinning. "And what could be more worth it?"

Ignoring the drivers who swore and swerved around her double-parked car, Kate helped me lift the sopping Woodrow into her pristine back seat, soaking her shirt in the process. Kate was a friend I trusted completely when it came to inflicting Woodrow's infirmities on her. She was a dog person who couldn't have a dog because her husband, Wonderful George, had been chased and bitten too many times on his morning jogs. Kate loved Woodrow, and time and time again she'd proved it, carting us to the beach, not minding the sand, seaweed, and dog fur that accumulated in her car, bringing towels and water for Woodrow. She was who I'd been with when Woodrow's legs gave out after his last ocean swim, when after bounding in and out of the waves for an hour per usual, he was bringing me his ball and suddenly his hindquarters sank to the sand. Kate and I stood over him. "That can't be good," I said. "No," she agreed. She helped me get a towel under Woodrow's belly as a sort of sling and we carried him back to her car, and in her passenger seat I'd ordered his first harness.

But Kate, like me, had some of that Churchillian stubbornness. She didn't see any reason why, just because the Atlantic surf was too challenging for Woodrow's old legs, he shouldn't still be able to swim. She kept showing up and chauffeuring us to Westport, where she'd found a pond hidden among some inland dunes. It was governed by squadrons of swans, who floated toward us in menacing formation but glided away at the last minute, allowing

Woodrow into the water. For the first couple of steps I had to hold on to his harness, and then the buoyancy took over and he was able to paddle toward his ball. In the water Woodrow had mobility that he no longer had on land.

We hadn't gone to Westport since May, though, for obvious reasons—Woodrow had barely been able to move from his bed without my assistance. I was feeling dubious about his prospects even in the swan pond. "I'm not sure it's safe for him to swim," I said as Kate navigated the surly traffic on I-93 South. "Maybe we should just take him to Partner's?" This was the bookstore-café we always went to after our excursions, where Woodrow lay on the weather-beaten boards of the porch to dry off, the sand rising out of his fur like cream from milk, and the patrons stepped over him and stopped to pet him, the kitchen staff calling "Woodrow!" from the pass-through window and sending out his own little rasher, in a cardboard boat, of bacon.

"Oh, he'll still get his bacon," Kate agreed. "But I have something special planned for us."

"What?"

"You'll see," she said.

When we reached Westport, Kate took the familiar route toward the ocean and the swan pond but bypassed them both. She turned instead onto a new road that took us out onto a causeway, which grew narrower and narrower until it was one-lane, bordered on either side by a steep seawall. Waves pounded the rocks, sending up spume and spray; if anything, this looked rougher than the regular beach where Woodrow had first lost his sea legs. "Where are we going?" I asked. Kate just smiled and drove us into the parking lot where the causeway terminated, like the eye of a needle. We had reached the end of the continent.

We were so far out that it was foggy, the ocean creating its own weather system. The windows grew gray and opaque. Kate rolled them down, and sea mist drifted into the car; I heard Woodrow struggle up in the back seat to lift his snout and do sniffs, then start to cry when he smelled the salt water. Kate inched forward, past some parked cars, and came to a stop before a flat ramp.

"There!" she said. "Boat launch. I found this the other day on a scouting expedition. I can drive out onto it, and it'll be easier for Woodrow to get out. Do you need help, or shall I go park?"

"No, I've got it," I said. "Thank you, Kate. I think you've found maybe the only place in the world where Woodrow can get into the ocean. Thank you so much."

"You're welcome," she said.

I lifted Woodrow out of the back seat and helped him hobble down to the water. It was low tide, so the waves, fierce on either side of the sea wall, here lapped gently at the shore. I'd been a little worried that we'd be told to leave; dogs weren't allowed on Massachusetts public beaches until October, when the season was over. But because of the warm fog there were scant other people here today, only a couple of fishermen feeding their lines out into the waves and a few die-hards in beach chairs dipping into their coolers, towels draped over their legs. One of them, a woman with a Koozie that read ROSÉ ALL DAY!, called, "How old?"

"Almost fifteen," I called back, my voice flat and muffled in the fog. She toasted us with her drink.

Woodrow meanwhile was nosing along the shoreline, sniffing shells and his favorite, seaweed. I guided him toward the water and we waded in. Kate had brought tennis balls with her, and I tossed one now, a few feet away; Woodrow paddled toward it, his fluffy undercoat lifting for extra buoyancy the way it was supposed to. But his legs were too weak; he sank like a stone. I grabbed for his harness handle.

"You're all right, Kooks," I said, "I've got you." I walked into the water with him, waist, then chest, deep. Woodrow snagged the ball in his teeth and rounded toward shore, a process that had once taken only a second and now was like watching the *Titanic* make a turn. Even with me holding him up, water got in his throat. He gagged.

"Okay, Kooks," I said and got him back to shore. Woodrow lay down on the sand, letting the waves wash up around him. He ejected the tennis ball at me and stared fixedly at it: *Get it, Mommoo.*

"Oh, I see," I said. "I understand how this is going to go."

For the next hour, Woodrow lay among the seaweed clumps and shells resplendent as a mer-king, shooting his ball at me while I fetched it from the water and tossed it back to him. It reminded me a little of when he was a puppy and I was teaching him to retrieve, a process that consisted of my throwing the ball, then running to get it while he watched: *This is a silly process, Mommoo, but whatever makes you happy.* Now Woodrow was as obsessive about the ball as he'd learned to be, only I was the one in the water. He caught it and spat it out at me and caught it again, sandy and stinky and happy as a clam.

Kate had come to stand on the beach and watch us, taking pictures; every so often Woodrow ejected the ball at her, too. "For me?" she said, stooping to pick it up and toss it to me. "Thank you, handsome." The woman with the Koozie wandered down to join us, offering us some wine.

"I had one that lived to be almost that old," she said, her eyes wistful. "God bless him. Look how happy he is."

He was. He was in his element; there was nowhere Woodrow was more joyous than in the ocean. We played until the tide started coming in and the waves washed up around his neck; then Kate went to get the car. I sat on the bench next to Woodrow, my arm around him as he happily gummed his sandy tennis ball, and thought about when he was younger and I'd taken him to the beach every winter weekend, the North Shore, Manchester by the Sea. No matter how cold or gray it was, we went, in December, in February. Often we were joined by my friend Kirsten and her Saint Bernard Gracie, at the big off-season dog party that reminded me of the one in the children's book *Go, Dog. Go!* Dogs of all colors, shapes, and sizes raced jubilantly up and down the sand, cartwheeling in and out of the waves. *I'm free! Lookit me! I'm FREEEEEEEEEEEEEEE!* Woodrow retrieved his ball, of course, from where I hurled it with the orange Chuckit! throwing stick, fifty yards out beyond where the waves broke. He plunged into them again and again, not wanting to stop even when he was visibly shaking. One January day the surf was so high that he was the only dog in it; "Whose dog is *that*?" I heard another owner ask in horror, and I realized belatedly that maybe it hadn't been such a good idea to let Woodrow swim in ten-foot waves. He was riding the crest of one now, his legs visible through the gray-green water, struggling valiantly to keep him afloat, and I held my breath: What if the wave dumped him? What if he hurt himself, broke his neck or back? But he rode it in with the assurance of a master surfer, emerging from the foam sleek and dripping. He spat the ball at my feet and stared at it. *Again, Mommoo. Again.* That evening I watched him sleep, this creature I had domesticated, whom I walked on a leash and fed from a bowl on the floor, and marveled that today he'd braved and conquered elements no human would dare attempt.

That night I woke abruptly, alerted not by a *yark!* but a smell: the strong scent of seaweed at low tide. I knew immediately what had happened: another Poopsplosion. Except this one was an Atlantic-splosion; half the ocean, it seemed, sand and salt, had sprayed out of my dog. "It's okay, Kooks," I said as I cleaned him up; I'd gotten good at it by this time, using rags I kept in a plastic-lined laundry bag next to his bed, rolling him this way and that to replace his blankets with fresh ones. "It happens to everybody sometimes. And it was worth it, wasn't it?" A friend had once sent me an article from the satirical paper the *Onion*: "Dog Has Best Day of His Life for 1000th Straight Day!" The piece chronicled the dog's intense joy at having once again received a piece of bacon from the man who smelled like cigarette smoke!, at being scratched!, chasing the cat! It was a spoof, but it was also true, and it was one of the best things about having a dog: It was so easy to make him happy. No matter how lousy a day you'd had, you took the dog for a walk, fed him, gave him some treats, and the dog was happy, so it was a good day. Every night, still, before I said, "Mommoo loves you more than anyone in the uni" and went up to the loft, I sat with Woodrow and recounted the nice things we'd done that day: seen our friends, had dinner, sat on the bench . . .

"We went to the beach today, didn't we, Kooks," I said, once Woodrow was clean. "Who swam in the ocean today? Who? Was it you? You did, didn't you? It was such a good day." I had thought Woodrow would never swim in the Atlantic again. Kate had given us an incomparable gift: she had given us the impossible. "Today was the best day ever, wasn't it, Kooks?" I said, petting Woodrow's head. It was still slightly damp, smelling of seaweed. "Yes. It was."

Woodrow and the Ladies

One afternoon we are on the bench when a phalanx of young women sweeps down the Mall toward us. Woodrow, fast asleep, wakes immediately. He sticks his snout into the air, sniffing. His jaw drops open in a wolf grin. *A sorority, wouldn't you agree, Mommoo?* "I think you're right, Kooks," I tell him. These ladies are vibrating with youth and vitality, their skin tanned and long hair streaked from the summer sun, in short shorts and wedge espadrilles that make their legs look even longer. They're in peasant blouses, diaphanous print shirts, sunglasses, and fedoras. I shut my iPad and sit back. I know what's coming.

"OHHHHHHHH," they say as one, spotting Woodrow. They flow toward him like an amoeba, exuding love and fruity shampoo. "Oh my goooooodness, we LOOOOOOOOVE you! Can we say hi to your dog?" Woodrow struggles to his feet, ignoring me when I jump up to help him. *Back off, Mommoo. I work alone.* "Ooooohhhhhhhhhh," the ladies say, as Woodrow stands wagging before them. "What's your name, handsome?"

"Woodrow, the George Clooney of dogs," I say.

They squeal. "The George Clooney of dogs! That's SO right. He's soooooooo cute!" They engulf him, petting and cooing. My dog disappears from sight.

What's your secret, Woodrow? my friend Stephen has commented every time Woodrow appears on social media with beautiful women—which happens on a fairly regular basis. I'd pay a lot to know.

I'm sure you would, Mister, I write back as Woodrow. I wish I could tell you, but it's just a certain je ne sais quoi. I could tell Stephen—and others who inquire after Woodrow's legendary ladies' man status—about a new secret weapon in Woodrow's arsenal. It's called sildenafil, a drug prescribed by Dr. Zarin to increase Woodrow's lung function. I didn't think anything of it until I tried to refill the medication at my local CVS when it ran out, and the pharmacist called me personally.

"I wanted to make sure you want this refilled," she said.

"Of course," I said. "Why wouldn't I?"

"Well, the cost," she said. "I wanted to be sure you were aware of the cost."

"How much is it?" I said, mentally sighing, adding another $100, $150, to the already robust column of figures in my head, the amount Woodrow's medications cost me every month.

"It's thirteen hundred dollars and fourteen cents."

"What!" I said. "You must have the wrong prescription."

"No," she said, "it's sildenafil. Its common name is Viagra. Since your dog doesn't have insurance, that's what it costs per refill. Do you still want it?"

"No, thank you," I said. I hung up and called the Angell, where the pet hospital replenished Woodrow's Viagra prescription for $73. It was quite a markup, and I imagined every man of a certain age in Boston standing in line at the animal hospital, saying when he reached the pharmacy counter, *Uh, yes, this scrip's for my . . . dog.*

But I don't tell Stephen this, or anyone else. It's Woodrow's secret. And honestly, he has never needed Viagra anyway. Like the lady in the Maybelline commercial, he was born with it, his Woodrow magnetic appeal to the ladies. When he was eight weeks old, I was waiting in line for coffee at Starbucks and glanced out the window to see Andy's red cap completely eclipsed, as he stood with puppy Woodrow, by a sea of ladies.

Now, as I do every day, I watch my old dog get love and accolades. I ask if I can take a photo of Woodrow with the ladies for his Instagram account. I say "Bacon!" when they assemble themselves around him like a chorus line, and they all laugh. Woodrow, too, is smiling broadly. Then I take out my iPad again as they give him final pats and kisses and flow off, calling "Bye, Woodrow!," down the Mall.

September

LOVE THY NEIGHBOR

On September 30, Woodrow turned fifteen. I could hardly believe it. In May, when his heart failed, I'd prayed he'd make it a week, then a month. The week my mom passed, I'd sat in the Blue Pearl Clinic in Minneapolis and begged for just another year. Now he had outlasted not only what I'd asked for but everyone's expectations, and I dared to think: Christmas? Maybe? Meanwhile, I threw a party.

I'd always celebrated Woodrow's birthdays. They started out simple affairs that became more elaborate each year, like the hats in Dr. Seuss's *500 Hats of Bartholomew Cubbins*. At first Woodrow got a slider for every year of his life, plus one to grow on. By the time he reached double digits, that was a lot of hamburger, so I switched to meatballs, a whole tray of them with candles blazing in each one. For his fourteenth birthday, a very respectable milestone for a Lab, we'd had a casual gathering on the Mall of all the neighbors and their dogs. This was different. Woodrow had defied the odds. He'd evaded death. He was 105 years old in dog years. He deserved the bash to end all bashes.

I sent texts to all the friends and neighbors who kept us company on the bench—and also basically anyone who had known Woodrow, ever.

WOODROW IS FIFTEEN!
PLEASE COME CELEBRATE WITH US
ON THE BENCH
SEPT. 30TH, 6 PM
CANINES & HUMANS WELCOME
CHAMPAGNE AND BACON WILL BE SERVED!

I bought a case of brut and six pounds of bacon. I got balloons with paw prints on them and biodegradable cups and plates and a button that said BIRTHDAY BOY! I may or may not have spent several insomniac hours googling dog birthday banners, piñatas full of Milk-Bones, exorbitantly priced carob cakes (because dogs are famously allergic to chocolate). In the end, I refrained. I had *some* boundaries.

On the big evening, I helped Woodrow into the tuxedo collar he always wore to host parties and took him out to his bench. We moved even more slowly than usual, since I was laden not only with his harness but shopping bags, clanking with booze and bacon in Pyrex. Woodrow WHUMPED down in his usual spot as I unpacked everything, pinned the Birthday Boy badge to his collar, tied the balloons to the bench. Never one to resist a tiara, I put on one that read HAPPY BIRTHDAY! People walked past and smiled and some called good wishes to Woodrow, but none were our friends. As the sun went down, my spirits sank with it. I started to feel foolish: What if nobody came?

Then I saw Jacqulene at the end of the block, Rizzo straining on his leash toward us. "Oh thank God!" I said. "We're so happy to see you. I wasn't sure anyone would show up."

"I got hung up at work," Jacqulene said. "We would never miss Grandpapa's birthday, would we, Rizz?"

Rizzo touched snouts with Woodrow—*How are you this evening, Grandpapa?* Woodrow: *I am fair, young Jedi, fair to tolerable, but the human is making an awful fuss about something.* Rizzo sat next to Woodrow and wagged expectantly, so I took out the bacon.

"Is this what you want?" I asked. Woodrow pushed himself up, too. Four identical black eyes looked at me with undisguised impatience and lust. Four strands of drool began to stretch toward the ground.

"How are you at opening champagne?" I asked Jacqulene.

After that, in the way of parties, everyone arrived at once. Our upstairs neighbors Jamie and Jamie with their rescue Lab Cici. The top-floor guy Mike, with Zoe, who was not friendly to anyone but Mike. Sarah and Harriet— Sharriet—both wearing pink peonies for the occasion.

Monique, Paul, Amelie, and Stella arrived with Cashew, their goldendoodle, who still had not heard of the #MeToo movement and nosed everyone in intimate places. Allison and her elegant pointer Atticus. Deb with Big Sam the rare red fox Lab, who at 110 pounds was well named. Eileen with fierce eight-pound Spike, who wasn't. Mary with "little treat whore" Lucy, who like Woodrow was an elder and kept us good company on the bench most days. I once read that the people you spend the most time with are your closest friends, and these neighbor-dog parents had become, over the past four months, my tribe. Yet the partygoers were not limited to bench regulars: people who'd known Woodrow since puppyhood came. His godmother Cecile, who'd been the first human outside of me, Andy, and the breeder to hold him; Erin, who'd brought us Frosty Paws earlier that summer, and her three kids. The DeVeers, driving with their daughter Miss Amelia all the way from Georgetown, an hour north. Casey, Woodrow's current dog sitter; Sara and her husband, recording the party for posterity and Instagram. From all directions and chapters of Woodrow's life they came, streaming toward us with gifts beneath the big trees.

Woodrow sat by the bench as the melee swirled around him. He looked at me, eyes shining: *I don't know what is going on, Mommoo, but we should do this every day!* "I agree, Kooks," I said. I circulated with champagne, Monique with mulled wine. The dogs milled around in the dusk, barking, bowing, wagging, snouting people indiscriminately. Presents piled up on the bench, shopping bags I recognized from Polka Dog and The Fish & Bone; five-pound sacks of carrots for Woodrow's crisper drawer; stuffed animals, vegetables, and desserts, including a cake that when squeezed played "Happy Birthday" for about twenty minutes. Rosalie, Erin's youngest daughter, hopped up onto the bench. "People and dogs!" she shouted. "It is time for refreshments! Everyone must be suspected and prepared!" She opened the Tupperware and started throwing bacon into the crowd; the area around the bench became a feeding frenzy, a mass of eddying canine bodies, flashing eyes, snapping teeth. Monique elbowed me in the side. "Thanks a lot," she said wryly as Cashew swallowed a whole rasher of bacon. "We'll all be out emergency-walking them later, in our pajamas."

It occurred to me that I hadn't seen Woodrow in a while, so I went to find him: he was still in his usual spot, buried in a drift of gifts. He was panting happily, watching the activity like a spectator at a tennis match. I joined him on the pavement, sitting amid the toys with my arm slung over his back, and as everyone around us ate and drank—the dogs were by no means the only ones consuming the bacon—I thought of the first collection of friends we'd had like this, in Woodrow's first dog park on Beacon Hill. It wasn't an official dog park; it was a little pocket of asphalt hidden from the street by a tall iron fence, its only charms two concrete chess tables, the ubiquitous wooden benches, and some sad ginkgo trees. But because it had a gate you could close, all the neighbors with dogs congregated there, and it was where Woodrow first learned to retrieve—or rather watched me throw the ball, then go fetch it, grumbling "I bet Hemingway didn't have to deal with this." He had his first kiss in that park, with a Bernese mountain puppy he nuzzled through the fence. He earned his first nickname, Buckethead, because of his habit of picking up the white cleaning pail, flipping it over his head, and running blindly in circles, bashing into the walls. He made his first friends: Gilly the Jack Russell terrier; Sally the ancient, gentle gray pit bull. And in the way of people whose lives intersect several times a day, the owners and I made friends, too.

We were a loose constellation about as different demographically as you could get, with one common denominator: our love of our dogs. Every morning and evening we drifted into the park, holding to-go cups, conversing in a casual, often-interrupted way about weather, politics, and our pets' digestive systems. I had become the person I swore I'd never be: somebody who talked about poop. Gilly's owner was Sarah, a russet-haired dog trainer with a voice like Foghorn Leghorn and a laugh to match. Sally belonged to Dave and Russ, who wanted to be married long before the Commonwealth granted them the right. Phyllis and her dog Buddy labored up Beacon Hill every day from the housing project down the street. A dog park is the original republic; we were as democratic as they come. It was the real-life *Sesame Street*: it didn't matter if you were old, young, male, female, somewhere in between, black, white, LatinX or Asian, gay, straight, rich, or poor: all you had to do to belong was show up and bring your dog.

However, not everyone was so fond of the park. We had a set of neighbors in one of the bordering buildings who weren't so pleased by their view of the neighborhood pack. Every so often, as we stood with our cups of coffee or wine, we'd hear a window rumble up and an angry Oz-like voice shout: "Get those wild animals on leashes! I'm calling nine-one-one. You're breaking the law!" *Bam!*, the window slammed down. Shortly thereafter a squad car would pull up, and a pair of Boston's finest would enter the park to find not the vicious dog-fighting gang they'd been called to corral but a bunch of happy retrievers and rescue mutts galumphing in circles. The BPD would stay a half hour to chat about their own Buddies and Macks, then issue verbal warnings they knew we'd ignore and depart. It was an arrangement that suited everybody.

Except the irate neighbors, and unfortunately, they were well connected. One morning Woodrow and I arrived at the park gate with our coffee and tennis ball to find it . . . gone. The gate had been removed in the night. It had simply vanished off its hinges. And just like that, our community was dismantled, too. With the gate gone, the dogs could run past us into the street and be hurt or killed, and although it took us a little longer to disappear, one by one, the dog park friends drifted. The trainer moved with Gilly somewhere, nobody ever found out where. Dave and Russ and Sally went to Santa Fe. Phyllis's COPD wouldn't allow her to walk to a park farther away, so she and Buddy just looped the block and went home. Over time the park filled with needles and syringes, people congregating in the shadowy corners. Nobody cleaned up. One day when I walked Woodrow past, I saw a guy asleep on one of the benches, and the smell of urine was overwhelming. Vials cracked underfoot. I wondered if the cranky neighbors were happy now, if they were pleased with their plan of urban renewal, the changes they had wrought.

Woodrow and I moved away ourselves, across the Boston Common to the Back Bay, and I didn't think of that first park much anymore. But it occurred to me now, watching Monique light candles on the special expensive carob cake she had bought, that the pocket park was not an anomaly. Community was a constant. People of goodwill would continue to find each other and assemble; kindness would triumph over sour pettiness every time. Generosity had followed me and Woodrow across the Common—in fact everywhere we went. And I was grateful.

It was full dark now. We sang happy birthday to Woodrow, the candles blazing on the cake. Woodrow wolfed down the first slice, as was his due. After that, the party broke up. Casey and the DeVeers helped me collect the empties for recycling and pack Woodrow's loot into shopping bags. They bulged, full to the handles. I was, as usual, returning inside with more than I'd come out with. We stood and waved to people as they walked off down the Mall, disappearing into the night, calling, "Goodbye! Happy birthday, Woodrow! Goodbye!" As I helped Woodrow inside, I didn't feel lonely at all. I knew I'd see many of them again in just a few hours, as Monique had predicted, walking our bacon-stuffed dogs in our pajamas.

The Bacon Boys

As time wears on and Woodrow becomes more and more an elder statesman, he tolerates puppies less and less. Puppies are fools, and Woodrow does not suffer fools gladly. This is a new thing. Woodrow has always been amiable and social, liking other dogs—until these last months by the bench. Once upon a time, Woodrow would have been patient with the young whippersnappers jumping all over him, licking his teeth if they were subservient, batting him with their clumsy not-yet-grown-into paws. Now, as he lies on his patch of dirt next to the bench, having difficulty breathing, his joints hurting, if a pup gets too close or obstreperous, Woodrow shows teeth. If that doesn't work, he snarls. Sometimes he nips. I apologize, saying Woodrow is a cranky old man and not feeling his best, and the pups' owners apologize as well, dragging their hyper charges away. "It's fine," they say, "somebody has to teach him to behave."

The exception to the rule is Rizzo. Rizzo is the one-year-old black Lab we call Woodrow's Mini-Me or, alternately, young Jedi; he lives about eight blocks away with Jacqulene. Both Rizzo and Jacqulene are beautiful physical specimens. Rizzo is such a gorgeous English Lab, with his muscular body, traditional boxy head, and shining fur, that when Jim first glimpsed Jacqulene walking him as a puppy, he ran out of the apartment in his boxers to ask where she got him. Jacqulene is tall and tan and young and lovely, like the girl from Ipanema, a weight lifter who favors crop tops, with long brown hair and oceanic blue eyes. She also has a poetry MFA, but when men drive past in cars, it's not her master's degree they're seeing. There's a lot of catcalling and whistling when Jacqulene and Rizzo are around.

Like most young Labs, Rizzo is extremely athletic and energetic. He's in his element racing up and down the Mall with a full-size tree branch in his jaws. If he sees a squirrel or bird, his whole muscular body stills, then quivers. He has comically big feet, as oversize as Mickey Mouse's gloves, and people always exclaim, "Oh, he's going to be HUGE. Look at those paws!" He hurtles at you like a cannonball, the same force and velocity, his head the same size and twice as hard. At ninety pounds, if he charges you, he'll knock you flat.

With all his potential for wreaking bodily harm, Rizzo is exactly the kind of careless youngster my cranky old man should abhor. But Rizzo's the exception to Woodrow's no-tolerance-for-pups rule. Whenever Rizzo sees me, the human treat dispenser, he breaks into a racehorse run, and I brace for impact—but when he notices Woodrow, he slows, then stops. He sniffs Woodrow, nudges him gently with his snout. *How are you today, Grandpapa?* Woodrow, gazing into the distance, ears back, regal: *Passable, young Jedi. Can't complain.* Rizzo: *Glad to hear it, Grandpapa. Glad to hear it.* Rizzo eases down next to Woodrow, adopting whatever pose Woodrow is in. Sphinx pose: chest out, head high, surveying the Mall for approaching admirers. Lobster pose: snout flat on pavement, tragic eyes, arms spread in a Y. Bookends: lying on their sides, legs outstretched. They remind me of the poster of the Lab Alphabet, the way these retrievers of ours contort their bodies into shapes that look like letters. Two of a kind.

Never has their similarity been more apparent than the day I introduce Rizzo to bacon. Jacqulene, a much more conscientious dog mom than I am, is not in the habit of giving her Lab fatty, salty, potentially carcinogenic meats. Woodrow, on the other hand, is well acquainted. He was weaned on pig ears. Our friend Kate routinely brings him so much pork she's known as the Bacon Lady. Whenever he returns from the vet after an emergency visit—for instance, after the brain-tumor scare—he gets a whole pound.

My friend Stephen Kiernan has just visited with two packages of Oscar Meyer's finest, which even for Woodrow—and even with me eating some of it—is a lot. I bring half in Tupperware out to the Mall. Woodrow assumes his position by the bench, and we lie in wait for Jacqulene and Rizzo. Rizzo barrels toward me, sees Woodrow, puts on the brakes, sits next to Grandpapa. I pop the Tupperware lid. Elder and youngster spring to instant attention. "Sorry," I say to Jacqulene. "I'm a pusher. Is it okay?"

"Sure, go ahead," says Jacqulene, resigned. "He'll have to learn about it sometime. I'd rather he get it from you."

We take turns tossing strips to the bacon boys. Four strings of drool fly from jaws. Two sets of teeth snap. It doesn't matter that Woodrow's more than ninety-eight years older than Rizzo in dog age; he's just as adept at snatching fried meat out of midair.

Rizzo's eyes are glazed, bulging: *Why has nobody told me about this before, Grandpapa?* Woodrow: *Stick with me, kid.* During this bacon orgy, you'd be hard-pressed to tell, unless you noticed the George Clooney gray on Woodrow's muzzle, who is the senior.

Finally the bacon is gone. Jacqulene and I show our dogs our empty hands and say "No more." The dogs sink to the ground.

Has this been here all along? says Rizzo. *Why do we not get this "bacon" every day, Grandpapa?*

Don't worry, young Jedi, says Woodrow. *I'll show you how to train her.*

He curls himself into a C shape, and Rizzo does the same, pushing his rump against Woodrow's for company. From above they look like two attached croissants, a Siamese Lab Rorschach. They lay their heads down on the grass and sigh in unison, sated, watching the world pass them by, moving only their eyes.

October

LET PEOPLE IN

As the year ticked into its final quarter, we moved into my favorite month: October. The summer swelter was gone, replaced by crisp air that smelled at night like fireplaces and was easier for Woodrow to breathe. The Copley Square Farmers Market offered cider doughnuts, and the foliage for which New England is rightly famous started its annual blaze. Every morning when Woodrow and I went out to the bench, we sat in an orange-gold cathedral. Once we emerged to find that the city had raked, and Woodrow turned to me, ecstatic about the crunchy piles taller than he was: *Look, Mommoo, LEAVES!* He thumped down in them and disappeared, only the wagging of his tail letting me know where he was.

But as the days got shorter and the nights longer, as the brilliant bulb of the September sun sank toward the equator and became something softer, I couldn't ignore the fact that Woodrow's age clock was again ticking forward, too. He was still managing the stairs, slowly. His breathing and heart rate were fine; in fact, after his last checkup, Dr.

Zarin had told me: "I shouldn't say this, but whereas with most congestive heart failure patients the best we can hope for is to arrest the decline, Woodrow's heart seems . . . better." Woodrow was still eating his chicken and rice, showering it all over the kitchen. He was still gumming carrots he took from the crisper drawer into dozens of damp fragments that stuck to my bare soles. But also, he slept. He had been taking long naps ever since hitting fourteen or so, his nineties in human years. Now he dozed most of the day, the times he was awake getting shorter and shorter. He slept on his beds, on his drop cloths. He slept outside next to the bench unless roused by some particularly appealing human or dog, at which point he thumped his tail once, then went back to sleep. He had stopped watching squirrels, even his favorite, Sauvignon Blanca; she frolicked inches from his snout and he didn't twitch an eyebrow. It was probably okay for him to sleep so much; it meant he was peaceful, comfortable. But I knew it for what it was, and as I sat on the bench and watched him, my iPad ignored on my lap, I thought of Hemingway's *Old Man and the Sea*: "He no longer dreamed of storms, nor of women, nor of great occurrences, nor of great fish, nor fights, nor contests of strength, nor of his wife. He only dreamed of places now and of the lions on the beach."

One day when we'd just come in from our morning bench sit, my agent Stéphanie called. "Hi Jenna," she sang, "how are you?" My agent is wickedly smart, diabolically charming, French, and fiercely devoted to closing the deal. Just as I'd always wanted to be a writer, she'd always wanted to be an agent; she had negotiated parts for her Parisian school-mates in their grade school plays, and she once brokered a foreign deal for my sophomore novel, *The Stormchasers*, while being wheeled into the hospital to give birth to her own second child. She'd been responsible for my life, my career, my dreams coming true, for almost twenty years—longer than many spouses have been together. I adored Stéphanie and was just starting to not be terrified of her.

"Checking in," she said. "How is Sir Woodrow?"

I told her. "It depends on the day," I said.

She sighed. "Ah, it is hard, it is so hard." She had been following Woodrow's health journey since the summer, when I called her upon returning home from the Angell and said that Woodrow was in heart failure, and I might not be able to make my JBC audition. It was amazing, re-ally, since Stéphanie was not a dog person. She'd encoun-tered mean dogs in childhood and been frightened of them—even of Woodrow, who when she first visited our apartment jumped on her with all the enthusiasm of his breed. But then one of her coagents brought a very elderly pit bull to work, and next time Stéphanie stayed with us, I came downstairs in the morning to find her playing tug-of-war with Woodrow and a sock. "Sir Woodrow and I, we get each other," she said, and we all had macarons.

"Listen," Stéphanie said now, "I know you are busy, so

I won't take much of your time. I really just wanted to see how you are holding up. How is your self-care?"

I sighed inwardly. Privately, I found the concept of self-care—like the advice to "Live your best life!"—somewhat tyrannical. A nice concept, but often difficult to execute. What was wrong with living one's most mediocre life and being content with it? Some days you could manage only to live your worst life and muddle through. Self-care was the same: when you were caretaking somebody in failing health, it was hard to get a massage or a mani-pedi or eat three full meals a day. String cheese was a lot more doable.

"I'm doing okay," I told her.

"Good, good," Stéphanie said. "Are you producing any pages?"

Again I suppressed a sigh. Since May I'd felt like *Apollo 13* reentering the earth's atmosphere, shutting down all non-essential systems in order to survive. "If I can take care of Woodrow, that's a good day," I said. "That's about all I can do."

Stéphanie sighed for me. "It is so hard," she said again, and then, "But that is what I mean, Jenna. You show up for everybody else. Your students. Your friends. Sir Woodrow. But when do you show up for yourself? And I don't mean just eating and getting sleep, although of course that is essential. I mean writing. You are a *writer*," she reminded me firmly. "That is what you do. And you are more connected to yourself, you are happiest, when you are writing."

"I know," I said. "But—"

"Listen," Stéphanie said. "I know you are exhausted. I know it must seem impossible to write the Great American Novel when you have been tired for months. But that is not what I'm talking about—although of course I would love pages," she purred. "You know I would love love love another book from you. But! I don't mean that. I mean just write *something*. Anything. A short story. An idea for a short story. Even in your journal. Just to connect you to yourself. You know what I mean?"

I lay back on the sheepskin rug with Woodrow. He put his old paw with its hoary claws on my cheek in his sleep. His breathing was quiet, even. Outside, the remaining orange leaves on our cherry tree shivered in the wind.

"Because, and I hate to say it," Stéphanie said, "because we all know he is your baby and you have been taking such incredible care of him, but *puh puh puh*, Sir Woodrow will probably not live forever. And I want you, Jenna, to get your systems in place now. I want you to start with something simple, two or three days a week—or, if that is too much, two or three hours. Put writing on your calendar. And ask your friends to help. Your people *love* you, Jenna. Don't just ask them for help with Woodrow. Ask them for help with *you*. If you can't leave him, which I *complètement* understand, ask them to come to you."

I was silent. I had set the phone on the rug and was letting Stéphanie's voice come from it, like Scheherazade.

I thought of Carrie Fisher in *When Harry Met Sally* saying, "You're right, you're right, I know you're right."

"Jenna?" Stéphanie persisted. "Do you hear what I am saying?"

"You're right, you're right, I know you're right," I said. "Okay, I'll give it a try."

"Promise?"

"Promise."

"*D'accord. Très bien.* I have to run, but I will check in again soon, all right? Bye, Jenna," she sang. "You're the best."

"No, you," I said, and Stéphanie chuckled and signed off.

As with much of my agent's advice, I knew it was excellent, but the concept of honoring it made me a little uneasy. I had never written well with anybody in the house—except Jim, barricaded in his own studio. It was partly a hangover from the creatively disastrous days of my young marriage, Sean popping his head in and out of my study like a cuckoo, demanding to know when I'd be done—but writing for me had never been a social event. All the way back to my early childhood, when I'd wandered our backyard spinning stories in my head, I'd been by myself. As an adult, I'd tried writing in cafés, but I was too prone to eavesdropping, and whatever my fellow diners said made it into my work. At retreats, I sat and listened to everyone else writing, then rushed to the table for soup, wine, and conversation when the monastic hours were over and we could talk again. In graduate school, I went to a bar down the street from Boston University, where for the price of a Diet Coke I could take up a table all afternoon—which I then spent smoking and watching the ice cubes melt in my drink. At other people's houses, while they scribbled or typed assiduously away, I wondered: How did they not get distracted? Would it be rude to help myself to more coffee? What kind of flowers were those, and where had Whitney gotten that awesome subway tile for her kitchen? I did produce pages during these adventures—and none of them was any good. I wrote best, to quote the Coen brothers' movie *Fargo*, in "total fucking silence." In my own home. Alone.

And yet. There was a human downside to all that generative artistic solitude, the precious prison of my own making. It was the ticking clock. For me, this wasn't biological, at least not in terms of children. It was the sound of what I feared was lifelong loneliness, the only sound in an apartment where no other person lived. The ticking clock—which was actually a clock I loved, an antique walnut wall model my dad had bought me from Nantucket for my thirtieth birthday—marked off the minutes and hours and days and months and years of sitting in a corner of my couch with a book on my lap, of dinners eaten cross-legged in front of the TV, of weekends blending into weekdays and all holidays the same. It was the sound in the background when one night I choked on a piece of chicken while eating the elaborate coq au vin I'd prepared for myself, and while I tried to cough it up, all I could think about was how embarrassing it would be to die alone from choking on a piece of chicken. When I finally hacked it up, I said "Oh, thank you, God"—and then, after a pause, started eating again. (It was really good coq au vin.) The clock ticked throughout: the clock, the clock, the fucking clock.

Woodrow, when he came along, provided a different kind of time: dog time. In the mornings, we got up and had breakfast. We went for three walks a day. In his youth, every night around midnight he got a burst of energy and brought out all his toys: sock monkeys from his closet collection; his stuffed animals and restaurant food; Super Pinky balls he squeezed between his teeth, making an ominous creaking noise, until they shot from the side of his jaw as if from a cannon; tennis balls he ejected with unerring precision at my feet. His needs were a governance beyond my own, his heartbeat—even if erratic now—the best company. But of course, Stéphanie was quite right. Woodrow's own clock, the age clock, was ticking forward, and when he slept, which was almost all the time now, the sound of my own ticking clock was still there.

So I did it. I invited people in. This was uncomfortable, though I wasn't quite sure why. I loved entertaining. I gave tremendous parties, smashing seventy-five people into my 750-square-foot apartment and inundating them with hors d'œuvres and liquor. My brunches, which started at noon, went on so long that once, at 8:00 p.m., my friend Kirsten rather plaintively asked, "May I have a snack?" But cracking open the daily routine: that felt hard. It was embarrassing, potentially. It was one thing to have a partner whose routines and eccentricities blended with your own, or to be a hostess or have weekend guests. It was another to let people see Woodrow's lazy Susan of meds on the kitchen counter, his orange chicken casserole in the fridge and drop cloths blanketing the floors; my underwear drying in the shower and manuscripts piled everywhere. What if my friends, despite being some of the kindest, most compassionate people alive, found our existence—the canine nursing home—pathetic?

But when everything in your life is up in the air, it's a good time to make changes. So much had shifted for me over the past two years: my mom's death, the dissolution of my engagement, Woodrow's declining health. Like any good Jersey girl, I now thought: What the fuck. I took Stéphanie's advice and decided to expose my little freak self to my friends, not really expecting they would take me up on my offer anyway: Who would drive in from the suburbs to hang out with me and an old dog? Erin and Cathy on Tuesdays. Mark and Jenna P on Wednesdays. Cat on Thursdays. That's who. They all came.

All week now, I had company. The writers arrived and shucked off their boots and hung their winter coats. They sat on my grandmother's stool or stood in the doorway of my tiny kitchen while I played barista based on the preferences I'd written on my chalkboard: coffee with heavy cream and sugar for Erin; nothing for Cathy (she brought her own concoction); double espresso for Mark; mint tea for Jenna P; anything with caffeine for Cat. We talked for an hour or so about what we were going to write, stating intentions for the day. Eventually we all sifted into positions we'd tacitly chosen: Cat in the corner of the long couch, where I took my meals; Cathy ditto; Erin in the study; Mark and Jenna P on either side of me at the dining room table so we made our own clock, they the 3:00 and 9:00 to my 6:00. Woodrow, who loved company—especially Cathy, who always brought him broiled organic chicken breasts—greeted everyone as they came in by grinning and huffing mollusk breath at them, then slept among us on his various beds.

It did not surprise me that I accomplished little on those days. I had book ideas. I had three novels plotted out on the bulletin boards in my study. But while my friends worked, I tinkered with those outlines or wrote notes about what I'd eventually write. Bringing a new book into the world takes a lot of energy, and I knew I didn't have it. Giving Woodrow the best care I could was my work now. Mostly I looked out the windows onto the Mall while my friends wrote, the afternoons growing dark earlier and earlier, the light withdrawing from beneath the big trees. The point, as I suspected Stéphanie had known, wasn't for me to miraculously produce a new novel under duress. The point was that with other people here, with their keyboard clicks and movements and murmurings, Woodrow's snoring beneath it all, I couldn't hear the ticking of the clock.

One afternoon in late October, on an Erin and Cathy day, instead of having lunch after writing, we helped Erin rehearse for the launch of her first novel, *Witches' Dance*, a week away. We gathered in the study, Erin sitting in my green velvet chair with her galley and pencil, Cathy and I listening and making suggestions. I tried not to get too verklempt with pride: Erin had been in my very first novel workshop almost twenty years before. As she was nearing the end of her passage, we heard a sound—*yark! yark!*—and looked over to see Woodrow standing in the middle of the room, beaming at us, twinkling all four of his remaining bottom teeth.

"Wow," said Erin, "I've never seen him in this room before. I'm so honored."

"He wants to hear *Witches' Dance*," I said.

"He wants more chicken," said Cathy. Cathy had lost her greyhound, Bo, a few years earlier, and her smiles at Woodrow always had a particular curve of tenderness, and sadness.

Yark!, said Woodrow, and WHUMPED down onto the carpet. We all laughed.

"That's my cue," said Erin, "I didn't realize it was so late." I stood with them in the foyer as they put on their parkas and boots and packed away their laptops. See you next week, they said as we hugged, bye, bye, see you soon, Woodrow! And as they left, departing into the frosty evening, I realized one reason it might have been hard for me to let people in: it was all the more lonesome when they were gone.

Yark!, said Woodrow, and I sighed. He needed to go out, which meant putting on all our gear and embarking upon our laborious journey down the stairs. "Okay, Kooks, give me one minute to clean up," I said as I took plates, mugs, and spoons to the kitchen. Where I found to my surprise that although we hadn't eaten after writing, instead listening to Erin's reading, my friends had left food for me anyway: Cathy's lentil soup, with a sleeve of Saltines; Erin's homemade soda bread and a pound of what we called the "damned Irish butter," so yellow and rich we were forced to eat it with a spoon. It was more than a meal. It would feed me for a week. "Aw, you guys," I said to the empty kitchen, which suddenly, actually, did not feel so empty at all.

Yark!, Woodrow answered from the study. "Ha," I said. "I hear you, Kooks." I realized what he'd been trying to tell me, tell us, and it wasn't that he wanted to hobble down into the cold and dark. *Ladies, there is FOOD on the counter.* I carried him in a plateful of the bread, with plentiful Irish butter.

Aly & Co

One evening I am sitting on the bench per usual, iPad open on my lap, Woodrow taking the breeze, when I hear somebody calling my name. I look around and see my friend Alyson Richman, the novelist, walking toward me, flanked by two men. It takes me a couple of seconds to realize that what I'm seeing is real, not a hallucination brought on by too little sleep, too many post-midnight *yarks*. Aly doesn't live in Boston; she and her family have a gorgeous F. Scott Fitzgerald house on Long Island, on the Sound. Yet here she is, waving merrily at me, drifting across the grass like a heroine from one of her own book covers: navy A-line dress, dark red hair in a gently waving bob. (Aly, like me, often writes about World War II.)

"Hello!" she calls. "I knew we'd find you here!"

"Aly?" I say. "Is that really you? What are you doing here?"

"We had a college interview for Z," she says, indicating her tall, handsome, dark-haired son. He towers over Aly, which is really saying something, since she's a willowy five eleven. "So I thought we'd come and surprise you and your prince. I couldn't remember your address, and I didn't want to give it away by asking, but I knew from Facebook the bench is on the Mall. So we've been walking up and down until now—we've found you!"

To her son and the other man, her husband Stephen, a very

smart, very wry lawyer, Aly adds, "This is Prince Woodrow—I told you about him and his bench, remember?"

I fold my iPad away and stand up to hug Aly, more embarrassed than usual about my dog-mom clothes. Aly, as ever, is impeccably elegant, and when I say as ever, I mean it. She and her daughter C wear matching mother-daughter outfits with gloves and hats to go on planes, because Aly writes about a bygone era in which people dressed for such occasions, and she believes they still should. To Aly, all of life is such an occasion. The soft waves around her lustrous face are created, I know, every morning, with old-fashioned curlers, and encircling her neck is a single strand of pearls.

"I can't believe you're here," I say again. I make introductions to Woodrow, who receives his company by WHUMPING dramatically over on his side in the grass. Z crouches next to him, petting him. Stephen watches, hands in suit pockets.

"How old is he now?" he asks.

"Almost fifteen," I say.

"Wow," he says. "That's really getting up there."

I know, I start to say, but Aly says swiftly, "Prince Woodrow is valiant! He will live forever."

She sits on the grass as well, her skirt a graceful swirl around her. "How is he doing?" she asks, stroking Woodrow's head.

"Fine!" I say heartily. Aly nods. She knows what this really means. Earlier this spring, I was supposed to have dinner with her when she stopped by Boston on tour for her new novel, *The Secret of Clouds*. But when she called me after her event, I had to beg off: Woodrow had just had an accident and I was cleaning it up, in no shape to suddenly switch channels and dress for a fancy restaurant dinner. With many other people, I might have invented a more seemly excuse: a migraine, a burst pipe. But I trusted Aly, and when I told her the real reason, adding, "Sorry, it's so gross," she said, "Not at all. Would it be better if I came by for tea? I'll bring it to you, you don't have to do a thing, I insist, and I also insist on staying only an hour." She came from her hotel in an Uber, with scones.

"I thought maybe we could take you out for ice cream," she offers now.

"That sounds lovely," I say, looking doubtfully at Woodrow. He is dozing under Aly and Z's stroking hands, side puffing slowly in and out like a bellows. He hasn't done his business yet, which practically guarantees an accident if we go in now. And even if we skip the meander around the Mall, it'll take me a good fifteen minutes or so to get him up the stairs.

Aly follows my gaze. "Or," she suggests, "we could go get some ice cream and bring it back to you."

"Oh, no, I can't let you do that," I protest. I am a little mortified by how circumscribed my life has become, which I didn't really realize until this minute. If I can't even get ice cream with friends who have come all this way to see me, my situation must seem pitiful indeed. "Let me just bring Woodrow inside. It'll take me a few minutes, if you don't mind waiting," I add. "We're moving at a pretty leisurely pace these days."

"How can we help you?" Aly asks, as I shake Woodrow gently

to wake him. "Stephen, Z, please help carry Prince Woodrow inside."

"I've got it," I say, but Stephen insists, and he accompanies Woodrow's and my slow progress across the Mall.

Stephen holds the building door for us and offers to carry Woodrow up the stairs. Even if he weren't in a gray suit, I wouldn't take him up on this. "Thank you," I said, "we've got a routine," and Woodrow hobbles gamely up the steps.

"This is your place?" Stephen says in my apartment. He surveys it, hands in pockets. "Congrats," he says, "it's great. Oh, you have Aly's book," he adds.

"I do," I say. Aly's new novel is featured on my shelf with a photo of us at a Florida event earlier this year, before Woodrow got sick. "I'm really proud of her," I say, and I'm happy for Stephen to see this is true, that since the visit was impromptu I had no time to stage this display.

I get Woodrow settled on his bed with extra water, his box fan, and his Stinky Chickie. He pants happily at me: *Mommoo, there were visitors!* "I know, Kooks, wasn't that wonderful?" I say. "Be back soon," and as I lock the apartment door behind me, I have a flash of when Woodrow was a tiny puppy and I was going off to teach, leaving him in his crate, and how terrifying that was: as though, without my being there every moment, some cataclysm was sure to befall him. Even now, all these years later, I still don't like closing the door and walking away.

Outside Aly and Z are still on the grass where Woodrow was lying, a mother-and-son impressionist painting. Aly looks up at me and smiles, but the expression is also a little wary. Not because of me or Woodrow but because of what Woodrow's age portends. The reason I trust Aly with the truth about Woodrow's infirmities is that Aly is a dog mom, too, to Tofu. Tofu is a tiny white Coton de Tulear—basically a powder puff—who when I stayed at Aly's house on tour climbed into my suitcase and slept there overnight. Aly dotes on her human children, Z and C, but Tofu is her baby. She carries Tofu around, scooping her up and cradling her against her dresses' elegant bodices, kissing her fluffy white head. That last event I had with Aly, in Florida, we went back to the hotel afterward and had piña coladas by the pool even though it was sprinkling a little and we were the only people outside beneath the heavy gray-bottomed clouds. It was such a luxury to spend the time together, to catch up each other's writing and lives, and I told Aly about Woodrow and asked after Tofu, and suddenly in the midst of giggling over some silly thing her dog had done, Aly's face creased, and she started to cry. "What is it?" I asked, alarmed, and Aly said, "I just can't stand to think of losing her, I love her so much it hurts! I can't stand to think that she's going to die!"

"Aly," I said. I couldn't help laughing. "You've got a ways to go. Tofu is *two*."

I know Aly will like strolling through the Public Garden, with its flower beds and fairy-tale blue bridge, gas lamps and swans, so I suggest we go to JP Licks on Beacon Hill. Stephen and Z walk a few paces ahead, one tall and graceful like Aly, the other stocky and dynamic in his suit. Aly links her arm in mine as if we were

French schoolgirls, not minding my worn-out yoga pants and Dr. Scholl's, my hair in a messy Katniss Everdeen braid. "How is Prince Woodrow, really?" she asks in a low voice. "How are you?" I try to say *Fine*, but my mouth quivers and I nod and look away. Aly squeezes my hand. She knows.

November

GIVE THANKS

My aunt Judy has a saying: If Mohammed can't go to the mountain, the mountain comes to Mohammed. Usually I traveled for Thanksgiving, to my siblings or, in past years, to my mom's, but this year it was out of the question. I couldn't leave Woodrow—not because his sitters, Casey, Alyson, Caroline, and Maddie, wouldn't take excellent care of him. They would; they always did. But his accidents and the demands of his very specific routine were a lot on top of his byzantine medication schedule and hauling him in and out of the house twice a day, plus hour-long bench sits in the cold. It was too much.

So the mountain was coming to Mohammed: my best friend Julie was flying in from Los Angeles. I was overjoyed. Julie was from Harvard, Massachusetts, a small town outside Boston, but she hadn't visited in twelve years, not since moving away for grad school. We'd met here, when I was teaching a short story workshop for Grub Street Writers, so long ago that I was still wearing glasses to look authoritative, not because I actually needed them.

(Now I did.) I was in my late twenties, Julie a few years younger, and when in class she wrote about being embarrassed at her dad's funeral by her weird preoccupation with her flaking pedicure, I thought: This woman gets it.

We went out that night to a dive bar and bonded over vodka tonics, a friend first date that became a ritual. We called ourselves the Bereavement Club, Membership 2. I had lost my dad that year as well, and we bonded over how peculiar death and dying were, how they weren't what you'd thought they would be. I'd always imagined grief meant wandering through a desert in black clothes, howling and tearing your hair, but instead, it came at you sideways. It made you messy. Julie called it "flail." Flail meant behaving like a lunatic despite your best intentions. You'd find yourself drinking much more than usual (me), getting divorced (also me), sleeping with inappropriate people (Julie and me). You'd go to a party and fill the guests' shoes, lined up at the door, with tortilla chips (both of us). You'd do a walk of shame home from a one-night stand in the guy's shoes because you'd lost your own, so you had to flop along like a clown in size 13s (Julie). You'd learn things people not in the club didn't know, things you never wanted to learn, such as how to write a eulogy for your parents. Or dress for the reading of the will. How siblings, not at their best anyway because death, could split further because money. How the family constellation you'd always known could blow apart under the force of grief, people exploding at one another or moving away, assuming different positions. How there was a hateful humor to death and dying as well; for instance, when I'd been carrying my dad's urn in a tote bag on Nantucket, en route to scatter his ashes off a boat, and my mom had said, "What've you got in that bag?" "Dad," I'd yelled, in front of the well-heeled shoppers on cobblestoned Main Street—"Dad's in the bag, Mom!" And how Julie's father, in the final days of his chemo, had eaten a whole tray of brownies she'd made, not knowing she'd baked pot into them.

Gabriel García Márquez wrote of one of his characters that he could see what was on the other side of things. That was Julie. She was the first truly honest person I'd ever met, and as a social worker, she found no behavior or situation too messy for compassion. She'd rescued her own dog, a Chihuahua mix named Indiana Jones, from the street in West Hollywood, with gaping wounds from a dogfight, and taken him in and nursed him even though her live-in boyfriend threatened to leave, then did. She was the person I told all the things to, the shameful and embarrassing and ridiculous things I never told anyone else, the things that made us human. Then we'd laugh about them. She was the perfect person to have for Thanksgiving always—and especially this year, with my increasingly infirm, accident-prone, eternally beloved dog.

When Julie arrived on Thanksgiving Day, I welcomed her by jogging down the stairs in my Mister Brisket Meat-Mobile T-shirt and leggings, hair in a bun, no bra or makeup, waving my arms wildly in the air. "I can't hug you," I said of the surrender position. "I just had my hands up a turkey's ass." We mime-embraced instead, and Julie lugged her suitcase up the stairs. "I think the turkey's poisonous, by the way," I added.

"Why do you think that, Puppet?" she asked. We called each other Puppet because of a student in that first writing workshop who told us she was a puppeteer, then said with great hauteur and hot indignation, "And there is nothing funny about puppets. WHAT IS SO FUNNY ABOUT PUPPETS?" In fact nothing *was* funny about puppets; as everyone knew, they were really fucking scary. "What's so funny about puppets?" Julie and I said to each other for years afterward, bugging out our eyes in fear.

"The turkey smells weird," I said, as we went into the apartment. Woodrow struggled to stand up from his bed. I had warned Julie about his condition, that he wasn't the dog she'd seen in previous years, that he was having a hard time walking and moving around and controlling his continence and sometimes eating. She went over to sit with him.

"What do you mean, the turkey smells weird?" she asked, petting Woodrow, who smiled his biggest Muppet-mouth smile. "It smells like turkey."

"Not when I took it out of the plastic," I said. "It smelled sour, like brine. I mean, it is brined. I never got a turkey prebrined before, and maybe that's how it's supposed to smell. But I also got it a week ago, and even though the butcher assured me it was perfectly fine to keep in the fridge for a week, I'm just worried it's poisonous." I did not add that between taking Woodrow out for that morning's bench sit and moving him around when he yarked, I had been googling "How long to safely keep turkey in fridge." The results were not promising.

"I'm sure it's fine, Pupp," said Julie, following me into my tiny kitchen and helping herself to a glass of water.

"I hope so," I said glumly. I opened the oven. We peered in.

"I think it smells like turkey," said Julie.

"I called the Butterball Turkey Talk-Line," I said.

"What did they say?" Julie asked. She sat on my grandmother's stool with her water, her back against the chalkboard where the writers' coffee preferences were written. She looked the same as always, a taller, sturdier choppy-haired Meg Ryan in a tank top, a stud twinkling on one side of her nose.

"They said, 'Did you get the turkey from Butterball?' I said no. They said then they couldn't be sure it was okay," I said. "They turkey-shamed me."

"Well, of course they did," she said. "If it wasn't theirs."

"But they said it would probably be okay. *Probably*," I said ominously.

"I'm sure it's fine."

"I really hope it's not poisoned. I would hate to have you come all the way here from California and then poison you."

"I wouldn't like that either," she agreed.

"Well," I said. I opened the oven again to see if anything had changed. Julie was right, it smelled like turkey, that once-a-year Thanksgiving fragrance, but I just couldn't be sure. "We'll see," I said, and shut the door again.

While we were having this conversation, Woodrow had maneuvered from his bed to the kitchen doorway. He lay on the threshold, smiling wolfishly at us, his front paws pushed under the rug, rucking it up in a way that would trip me if I weren't careful, in which case I'd surely brain myself on the counter and die.

"Look," I said to Julie. "Dangerfooties!"

"Wow, he got in here all by himself!" said Julie. "Way to go, Woodrow."

We saddled up to take Woodrow out. I had told Julie about this, too, how involved the process was: attaching his leash to his harness, filling my pockets with treats for enticement, our cautious progression down the stairs with me holding up Woodrow's back legs. Traffic stopped as we hobbled across the street, and when I waved, the drivers waved and smiled back. "That's so nice," Julie said. "Nobody would ever do that in LA."

Woodrow limped along, sniffing. One spot wasn't right, then another. The ground was frozen in uneven hillocks, and he stumbled. In the past couple of weeks he'd grown thinner—spiny, his vertebrae humping beneath his fur in a way I'd seen on other very old dogs. But he was still a big heavy guy, and whenever he almost fell and I caught him, my arm yanked in a way I felt all the way up to my shoulder. "Come on, Kooks," I said. I held him up while he peed and tried to steer him away from the bench, but he lay down in protest. "Sorry, Pupp," I said. Although Julie was in one of my parkas, not having any of her own in California, she wasn't used to winter anymore. The air smelled of fireplaces and felt like snow; the leaves were off the trees.

"It's okay," said Julie. "It's nice to be outside. I miss this kind of air."

I lifted Woodrow up. "Come on, old man," I said, "time to go poops, please." He investigated a tree or two, then headed back toward the bench. "Can you sit a minute?" I asked, "or is it too cold?"

"No, it's fine," said Julie. We sat on the bench. A couple strolling by stopped to say hi to Woodrow, crouched to pet him, asked how old he was, exclaimed when I told them. Woodrow's jaw dropped open in his big smile. The couple told us about their golden retriever, at home far away, then wished us a happy Thanksgiving. "Happy Thanksgiving," we said.

"Welcome to my life," I said after they'd walked away, looking back over their shoulders and smiling. "This is basically what we do all day, every day."

"Aw," said Julie. "I know. You told me. It's nice to experience it in person."

"I'm sorry about the poison turkey," I said.

She laughed. "Pupp, if you keep calling it that, I won't want to eat it."

"It's probably fine. Don't you think?"

"I think it's fine."

"I'm aware this is a *Waiting for Godot* conversation," I said, "and I know I'm obsessing about the turkey because I can't control bigger things, like Woodrow getting . . . more infirm. You know?"

"I know, Pupp."

"Thank you for being so supportive," I said, as Woodrow started trying to push himself to his feet, his front legs scrabbling in the dirt. I leaped up to help him. "Hold on, Kooks, I got you . . . I know it's hard to see him older," I added.

"It's fine, Pupp," said Julie, and kept us company as we circled around and around, me bent over to hold Woodrow up as he looked for just the right sniff spot to do his business. Julie offered to carry the double-bagged poop to the garbage can when he was done, and because she was my best friend, I felt okay about handing it to her and saying thank you. "Good job, Woodrow," she said as we went inside and I threw treats up the stairs to coax him up, one by one. She kept pace with us every step of the way, but I knew she was sad.

We had the Thanksgiving dinner around four, my friend Cecile, Woodrow's godmother, joining us. Cecile was a vegetarian who was therefore spared my conundrum about whether to eat the potentially poisoned turkey. I took a couple of slices to keep Julie company, joking that I'd wait a few minutes to see if she survived the first bites. She did, and I nibbled a bit of drumstick, but mostly I hid the meat beneath the sides and stuck to the brussels sprout salad, the mashed cauliflower with gravy. We drank wine and talked feminism while it got dark outside, the room increasingly illuminated by candles. Woodrow slept through the whole thing, on the rug near Cecile's feet. Once upon a time Thanksgiving had also been the best day ever, and then some. *Mommoo, a giant bird comes into the house and goes into the oven? We should do this every day!* One year Jim and I had watched Woodrow stick his entire head into the refrigerator and tug out a thawing eighteen-pound turkey, landing it on the kitchen floor with a THUD as we clapped and cheered. Now I had to wake him, trying not to startle him, to slip him a few scraps of skin.

The holiday weekend passed peacefully. We binge-watched a series on Amazon, braved the first blizzard of the season to go see a movie in a theater. I took Woodrow out beforehand, not wanting to come home to an accident, apologizing to Julie for the time it took. She was fine with it, of course, accompanying us outside in the snow. Woodrow sniffed and stepped cautiously. He didn't do his business, instead wanting to lie down on the frozen ground, and I felt that internal clang of alarm: his digestive rhythm was definitely faltering. I had the sense that his systems were shutting down. I spent much of the movie wondering if we'd return home to another accident and trying not to think of that quality-of-life calculator Dr. Mimi had sent me, the one meant to help owners decide when to put their pet down. *Are you unable to travel for fear of leaving your pet with a sitter? Are you afraid to leave your pet alone for fear of accidents? Is your pet mobile? Does your pet no longer enjoy his/her food?* More and more boxes were being ticked every day.

The next morning I came downstairs to find Julie awake before me, sitting with Woodrow on his sheepskin rug. He was lying with his head in her lap, and she was petting him. "I think he might be suffering, Pupp," she said. "It might be getting close to his time."

I stiffened. How could she? How could she say that in front of him? "He's fine," I said. "I mean, not fine, obviously he's really really old, but I would know if he were in pain. I would never let him suffer."

"I know you wouldn't, Pupp. But he just seems unhappy."

"He's not," I said. "I know it's hard for you to see him this way. He's had so many challenges. But I know him better than you, and I could tell if he were in pain."

"Okay. I know you know him the best."

"I do," I said. "I always promised myself if he couldn't

eat or do his sniffs, if he couldn't enjoy his life anymore, it'd be time to help him cross. But he can still do those things."

"Okay."

I tried not to think about Woodrow's failing digestive system, his lack of interest in the turkey. How he didn't want even carrots anymore, turned his head from the open refrigerator. How he had started to pee in the house as well as lose control of his bowels, and I'd find him in the kitchen or bathroom, having dragged himself to those hiding places, licking his chops in shame. And how I'd thought: This newly checked box will make our lives infinitely harder. I said, "I know you're trying to help. I appreciate your being here with us. But you know you and I have always had differences about how to treat pets. You grew up in a rural area with horses, you treat them like animals. My family doesn't do that. Our dogs are like our kids."

"That's true," Julie said, stroking Woodrow's head. He was dozing.

"So we have a difference of opinion about when to help them cross. They let you know. He'll let me know when it's time."

"He will," said Julie. She looked up at me. "I'm sorry. I didn't mean to make you mad."

"I'm not mad," I said.

I was furious. The rest of Julie's visit I could barely be

151

civil, and although I felt terrible about it, it was a relief when she left. I didn't want her negativity in my space, contaminating my dog. How could she have said that in front of Woodrow, that it was his time to go? What if she'd injured his will to live? That was so important, especially when he was challenged physically. Didn't she know he could hear her? Although—I had to admit—he probably couldn't. Woodrow's hearing had declined significantly as well, so I had to raise my voice and clap when I needed his attention, and he often startled when he realized I was in the room. Another box checked. My dog's body was shutting down more every day.

A few nights later I was lying in bed talking on the phone to Jim, Woodrow on his own bed beneath the loft. It had been a bad night. I had been cross with Woodrow. He had been yarking persistently: *Yark! Yark! Yark!* Every few minutes, so I couldn't eat, or read, or watch TV, without getting up to move him, or bring him water, or give him a treat. "No? That's not what you want?" Finally I took him out, even though we'd been out earlier. It was a miserable night, with sleet and freezing rain, blowing sideways so an umbrella would have been useless even if I hadn't needed two hands to handle my dog. Woodrow had once again had trouble finding a spot to do his business. He'd hobble a few steps, sniff, then want to lie down. "Oh no you don't," I'd said. "Come on, dog. You wanted to go out. Now go. I don't want another Poopsplosion."

I'd marched him around the Mall, up and down. Once he fell, and this time my arm jerked so hard I felt something snap in my elbow. Woodrow slid down onto his stomach in the ice and mud.

We went back inside without success. I dragged him up the stairs with my good arm. Usually I tossed a treat onto each step as a reward, and when I felt annoyed by this, I reminded myself that one day, when he was gone, I'd give anything for the chance to give him a treat. I wanted to be able to say I'd never missed an opportunity to make him happy. But sometimes, on the bad nights, I told him, "No, it's not time for treats. It's too late. You didn't go, you don't get treats." And he limped up the stairs nonetheless.

Tonight he wouldn't have wanted treats anyway. In just the past week since Julie had left, Woodrow's appetite had departed too; he was barely interested in food anymore. I managed to wrangle him into the apartment and unclip his harness, then shucked off my soaked outerwear. Woodrow had sunk down to his rug. He was looking into the middle distance, at the wall. I sat down next to him. "I'm sorry, Kooks," I said. "That was hard, wasn't it? That was so hard. I'm just so tired. I'm sorry I was mean to you. I'm so sorry." He licked my hand.

I told Jim this story, and I started to cry. Jim said what he always did, what all my friends said—that what I was doing was so challenging that my reaction was understandable and human. Nobody was perfect, and it was exhausting caring for a dependent elder; I shouldn't judge myself so harshly. He reminded me of being at his mom's rehab center and hearing one caretaker tell another, "You're burnt out. Go, go for a walk."

"And they're professionals," he said. "You're doing this all on your own, and you're not a professional."

"I know," I sobbed. "But I was mean. I was mean to Woodrow. I was dragging his poor old body around. And he couldn't help it. He didn't do anything wrong. He's just old. Oh, my poor dog," I said, and I cried and cried. I often cried when I was impatient with Woodrow; even in the midst of it, when I was trying so hard to stop myself and failing, I hated myself. I hated those moments more than anything. I hated meanness in people more than any other trait, and being mean to Woodrow was the absolute antithesis of the person I wanted to be. There was a popular folksy saying I'd seen on dog-mom T-shirts: *God help me be the person my dog thinks I am*. Woodrow knew better. He knew I could be cruel.

"You're being really hard on yourself," Jim said. "You're the best dog mom I know. Woodrow knows you love him more than anything."

"Thank you," I sobbed. "I know."

But I couldn't stop crying. It wasn't just about tonight's incident. It was something bigger, the knowledge bulking there and my refusing to let it in.

After I said good night to Jim and shut off the light, after I'd called to Woodrow "Mommoo loves you more than anybody in the uni, yes she does," I put myself to sleep the way I always did: by saying my gratitudes. It was a form of thumb-sucking, of meditation or counting sheep. Every night I recited a list, whispering it into the dark, of the things I was thankful for. I always started with: *Thank you, God, for my wonderful dog, the best dog in the universe.* I did that tonight, too. *Thank you for Woodrow. Thank you for Jim and his understanding. Thank you for Julie's visit, even though she pissed me off, and for her safe passage home. Thank you for my friends....* Usually I fell asleep while doing this, but tonight the list trailed off and I was still awake. I lay listening to Woodrow's breathing beneath me, and I was thankful.

The Lady in the Snow

In the first week of December, it snows again. A wind from the
north quickly scours it away, leaving icy crusts. Woodrow and I
move extra slowly outside, me planting my feet carefully so as
not to slip and take him down with me—or vice versa. During the
winter of 2015, Boston received a record seventeen feet of snow,
with drifts so high they obscured traffic lights and the mayor had
to chide residents about exiting their houses by jumping from
their second-floor windows. When we'd crossed Commonwealth
to the Mall that year, Woodrow had literally climbed over parked
cars: they were buried like mastodons in drifts beneath our feet.
He was jubilant that winter, never needing a leash because, with
the streets shut down, there was no traffic. Every night he zipped
and bounded up and down the Mall, digging his favorite ball—a
blinking red one—out of the drifts and bringing it to me like a
visible heart in his mouth. Now he looks wearily at the ice as if to
say, *Oh, not this shit again.*

One morning the first week in December we venture out into
fresh snowfall. It's still coming down, turning the Mall into the
set of *The Nutcracker.* The trees are lacy with snow. It's a beautiful sight. Woodrow limps straight to his bench, then lies down.
"Don't you want to walk around a little, Kooks?" I ask him. He

sighs and rests his head. I take a photo of him, the only black spot in a panorama of white.

I sit on the bench with him as long as I can take the cold, answering work emails on my iPhone, drinking the coffee from my traveler. Woodrow appears to be dozing. He sleeps all the time now, nothing unusual for a dog his age, but since Thanksgiving I've also found him lying in strange places: the kitchen, where he usually only goes for food; the bathroom, his belly pressed to the tiles. Twice more this week, he's had accidents—peeing again, which seems to trouble him more than the Poopsplosions ever did. "It's okay, Kooks," I tell him as I clean up. "It happens to everybody sometimes." But it has never happened to him before, and he licks his chops and looks away, ashamed.

Finally my fingertips in their fingerless gloves are glowing red with cold, and I can't feel my feet. It starts to flurry again. "Let's go inside, Kooks," I say. "You ready?" I check Woodrow to make sure he's breathing. I do this every morning now, when I come downstairs: tiptoe closer to look for the rise and fall of his ribs. Woodrow wakes now but just looks at me when I reach out to pick him up. "Come on, Kooks, give me a hand here," I say, and then I realize he has had another accident, a bad one that has turned the snow beneath him to slushy brown soup.

"Oh, Kooks," I moan. I try to help him stand so I can clean him with some snow and the waste bags I always carry with me, in a roll attached to the handle of his leash. But as soon as I lift him, he collapses again. If I can't get him up, I can't wipe him off, nor can I get him inside.

I'm trying to decide who to call for help, or whether I can leave him while I run into the apartment for a blanket to use as a sort of sled, when a woman materializes out of the snow. She's about my age, as best I can make out between the intensifying flakes. She's in traditional Boston winter garb: ski parka, woolen scarf and mittens, boots. A few brown curls escape her knit hat. Kind eyes squinting against the snow. Freckles. "Do you need some help?" she asks.

I start to say no—how can I ask a stranger to manhandle my poop-covered dog?—then reconsider. "I do, actually," I say. "He's an old guy, and he's has an accident. If you could just help me stand him up so I can clean him—"

"Sure," she says. With her mittened hands she lifts the rear handle of Woodrow's harness while I lift the front, and we prop him upright; then she stands holding him while I quickly crawl around in the snow, cleaning him as best I can. Woodrow tolerates it as if he weren't there, gazing into the distance.

"Thank you so much," I say finally, when he is mostly just damp. "I can take it from here."

"Are you sure?" she says. "Do you need help getting him inside?"

"Oh, no, that's okay," I say. I've got a good grip on Woodrow's harness handles now, and all that remains is to guide him across the street, then up the steps. "Thank you, though. You've been incredibly kind." I try not to look at the large brown puddle next to the bench.

"I know how it is with old dogs," she says.

"Well, thank you again," I say, and begin the cumbersome process of turning Woodrow around with his harness handles. "Come on, Kooks, let's go inside." He's walking unsteadily across the Mall when I realize that if I get the woman's name, I can thank her: write her a letter, send her a gift certificate, laud her extraordinary kindness on Instagram, something.

"Hey," I call, turning, "what's your—"

But she's gone. I stare and stare and there's nobody there, not even boot prints in the whirling snow.

December

LET GO

If Woodrow loved all ladies in human form, when it came to canines, he preferred his women on the larger side. His first girlfriend was that beautiful Bernese mountain dog, who even as a pup outweighed him by thirty pounds. His longer-lasting love was Gracie, my friend Kirsten's Saint Bernard. Woodrow had known Gracie since she was eight weeks old, when on a frigid winter morning Kirsten and I put on camouflage pants—calling ourselves, for some reason, the Dog Retrieval Team—and drove into the backwoods of New Hampshire to fetch baby Gracie from her breeder's trailer. Gracie's head was bigger than her body; she looked just like a Muppet, and Woodrow greeted her by pouncing on her and saying *Rrr! Rrrrrr! Rrrrrr!*, then savaging her neck while making high-pitched whining noises. Kirsten and I watched, hands on hips. "I think that's playing?" she said doubtfully. For years Woodrow showed his affection by tormenting his lady love, even when Gracie stood a foot taller than him and could have squashed him like a bug. Woodrow was a good host in his tuxedo collar but a bad guest, and every time we went to Kirsten's condo he corralled all of Gracie's bones, leaped onto the chenille sofa, and gnawed them, while Gracie stalked us, whimpering anxiously: *People! People! The black dog is doing something not right!* If Gracie didn't pay sufficient attention to Woodrow, he poked her with one of the bones sticking out of his mouth: *Rrrr! Rrrrr! Rrrrrr!* But in the Fells, the woods where we walked as a quartet every weekend, Woodrow and Gracie were equals, tearing through the trees, mucking through swamps, and leaping off cliffs into quarries, disappearing down the trail and emerging a quarter mile ahead, looking back at me and Kirsten as if to say: *What is TAKING you humans so long?*

It is sadly axiomatic that bigger dogs don't live as long as smaller ones, and by the time Woodrow reached fifteen, Gracie had been gone for a few years. She and Kirsten had relocated to Denver when Kirsten married a Coloradan. But Kirsten owned her own company and traveled regularly to Boston, so every few months she came to our apartment and camped on the couch, cooking inventive chicken dishes with me and invigorating Woodrow, who every time he saw her pushed himself up and tried to run around the room: *Rrrr! Rrrrr! Rrrrr!*

In the first week of December one of Kirsten's visits happily coincided with a reading by one of our favorite authors, Elizabeth Berg. Elizabeth's novels were my comfort food, and Kirsten loved her books as well. Since

Thanksgiving with Julie, I had grown increasingly protective of who I let into the Woodrow zone—I didn't want anyone to offer even the slightest suggestion that his time might be near. Things were, physically, hard enough. But Kirsten, like me, came from a Minnesotan pioneering background—I always said of her that if she ran over her foot with a lawn mower, she'd still show up at brunch with a hot dish, saying, "That's okay, I have another foot!" She was calm and capable in the face of hardships (once we exploded a Pyrex dish in my oven, then spent the evening drinking wine while we picked out shards with tongs), and thanks to Gracie, she knew what it was to have an older, challenged dog. She was, I decided, a safe overnight guest.

She arrived at the apartment with her suitcase and said hello to Woodrow. We relinquished him to Casey, and off we went to see Elizabeth. The reading was at the Lenox Hotel, where Elizabeth and the event hostess, literary fairy godmother Robin Kall Homonoff, asked after Woodrow's health, and many readers did, too. Apparently Woodrow had more followers on social media than I'd thought. I arranged with Elizabeth to come and meet Woodrow the following morning and accepted a doggie bag of prosciutto the hotel manager gave me for him (I didn't tell her that it was too rich for Woodrow, but I'd eat it). "People have been so kind," I said to Kirsten as we left, bracing ourselves against the December wind. "It's unbelievable."

"That's so nice," she said. "But you know, Jenna, I don't think it's unbelievable at all. Woodrow gives people something to root for."

We had a lovely dinner, and back at the apartment Kirsten got settled on the couch while I took Woodrow out. She offered to accompany us, but his walks had become even more difficult, since he kept wanting to lie down on the frozen ground. I set out guest towels and bade Kirsten good night, and Woodrow and I went out on our slow rounds.

At about one in the morning, just as I was going to sleep, I was jerked awake by a sound every dog owner knows: Woodrow was throwing up. "This is new," I muttered as I raced back downstairs. Except it wasn't: Woodrow had thrown up a couple of times that week, after eating, coughing up half-digested kibble. He'd also been drinking a lot more water, which I thought was maybe the culprit. "It's okay, Kooks," I said as I swapped out his sheets. "Everyone has a vomit moment sometimes."

I brought him some more water, told him I loved him more than anybody in the universe, and went back to bed. But I lay awake, alert to more gagging noises downstairs. When they came, I threw the blankets off. "What is it, Kooks?" I said. Woodrow was throwing up again, all the water he had just drunk.

This couldn't be good. I called Jim, even though it was two in the morning. I described Woodrow's symptoms.

"Do you think I should take him to the Angell?" I murmured into the phone—I didn't want to wake Kirsten.

"It's a tough call," Jim said. "Do you think that'll be more traumatic for him?" It had been difficult enough to maneuver Woodrow in and out of the Jeep when I'd had Jim to help me. Considering it was now hard to help him across the street, transporting him to Angell would be a significant challenge.

As we discussed the pros and cons, Woodrow threw up again. "I'll call Angell and ask them," I said, promised Jim I would keep him posted, and hung up.

As I had suspected, the on-call vet thought Woodrow's vomiting an ominous sign. "With his heart condition, I think it's best for you to bring him in," she said. "We'll take a look at him, find out what's going on."

And so I got Woodrow up. He didn't want to go. He resisted, gave me reproachful eyes: *Mommoo, we have already gone out tonight—TWICE.* It was true. I had taken him out before the Elizabeth event and again when we got home, hoping to avoid post-midnight accidents. "It's okay, Kooks," I told him, clipping his leash onto his harness and lifting him to his feet. "We're just going to go get you checked out, and then I will bring you back to your nice bed. I promise."

Outside it was flurrying again. Nothing else moved. I guided Woodrow toward the Jeep, but he pulled toward the bench, showing surprising strength. He didn't want to get into the car. He knew where we were going. "It'll just be a little ride," I said, "to the nice Angell. They will help you feel better." I opened the door to the back seat, dead-lifted Woodrow in. He was so weak that he lay in exactly the same position he landed in, unable to lift his head. I sat behind the steering wheel for a minute to let the engine warm up and collect myself. "I know that was hard," I said to Woodrow. "I'm sorry."

We drove to the Angell through the silent city streets. I put the back windows down a few inches so Woodrow could do sniffs. He didn't move. He'd been still since I'd gotten him in the car. "Almost there, Kooks," I said. "Almost there."

At the Angell a vet tech helped me lift Woodrow onto a gurney. I kept pace with him as they wheeled Woodrow back toward the double doors, through which I couldn't go. Woodrow looked straight ahead, ears back, scared, as he was zoomed away. He knew he was in trouble. "See you soon, Kooks," I called. "See you in a little while!" When the doors closed, I made it a few steps down the hall toward the ER desk to check in, and then I doubled over. I was crying so hard I couldn't stand up. For so long I had prayed that I would not be one of the people coming out of those doors with only a leash in my hand. But I knew, I felt, that we would not be leaving the hospital with a miraculous stay of execution this time.

I checked in at the front desk, then called Jim. "It

doesn't look good," I said. "I'll let you know as soon as I hear anything." We were both sobbing so hard it was hard to talk. After I let him go, I sat on a wooden bench. The waiting area had a Memorial Tree, a wall covered with plaques shaped like leaves, each emblazoned with the name of a departed pet and sentiments from its family. There was also a real Norwegian pine, which was more comforting. I lay down, looked up into its branches, and wondered who would be up at 4:00 a.m. My friend Stephen Kiernan. Unlike me, he was early to bed, very early to rise. I called him. "Oh, honey," he said, when I told him where I was. "What's going on?"

"I don't know yet," I said. "Will you keep me company until I find out?"

"Of course," he said. "Where in the hospital are you?"

I described the bench I was on, the Norwegian fir. "Good," he said. "Lie back."

I did, and he talked to me for a long time about many things. The Labs he had known and bred as guide dogs, especially the one he kept for himself, his old girl Maggie. Art. Books. He recited some limericks. His voice washed over me for hours in that fluorescent light, at a time of night and then early morning when nobody should be awake. *Of shoes and ships and sealing wax; of cabbages and kings; of why the sea is boiling hot and whether pigs have wings.*

A woman in scrubs was coming toward me. "Jenna?" she said. "Here with Woodrow?"

"The doctor's here," I said, sitting up. "I have to go."

"Good luck, hon," Stephen said. "I'm thinking of you and the gent in the tuxedo. Big love to you both."

I followed the doctor into a consulting room. I sat, and she sat across from me, an exam table between us. "I'm sorry," she said, "but the news is not good. Woodrow has a mass in his stomach."

I shook my head. "No, he doesn't," I said. "He's a cardiac patient. He has a bad heart."

"His heart actually is fine," the doctor said. "We ran an EKG. But he has a very large mass in his stomach. That's what's causing the vomiting. He's bleeding internally, and that's why he's so weak. I'm very sorry."

I sat there trying to process this. I kept shaking my head. "That can't be right," I said. "I'm sorry, I know I'm in shock, but . . . He has a bad heart. He's never had any trouble with his stomach. Are you sure it's not something else? Something he ate, maybe? Or bloat?" Even as I said this, I knew that if Woodrow did have bloat, a condition caused by Labs eating so enthusiastically their stomachs flip over, the only cure was surgery. And he was far beyond that possibility. But still. "A mass? In his stomach? I don't mean to be rude," I said, "but are you sure you haven't made a mistake?"

"I can show you," the doctor said finally. "I can take you back to him and let you feel it. If you put your hand on his stomach, it's palpable."

"Yes, please," I said.

The doctor took me back through the double doors and down a long hallway. "We don't normally do this," she said sternly. "But I want you to have no doubt in your mind about this. I have to tell you, I don't recommend you take him home."

I stopped walking. "What do you mean?"

"I mean I don't think he should be moved. He's in pain. We should euthanize him here. I'm sorry," she said. "I know this is hard to hear."

"I'm not prepared to do that," I said.

"I understand. But it's in his best interest."

"I have a doctor who will come help him at home. I've already arranged it," I said, which was true. Dr. Mimi and I had discussed the plan many times.

"I'm not comfortable with that," said the doctor. "I think after you see him, you'll understand why."

She ushered me through another set of double doors into the surgery area. Woodrow was on a metal table, part of his stomach shaved, an IV in his leg. Around us were more tables, cages with animals in varying degrees of distress, beeping machines. Woodrow was semiconscious, his eyes half closed and glazed. "Oh, Kooks," I said. I put my hand on his head. "Here I am. I'm right here."

The doctor showed me where the mass was, had me palpate it. It was the size of a grapefruit. I remembered now how Woodrow had wanted to lie down for the past few weeks, to put his belly in the snow or on the cold ground or cool tile in our kitchen. All that time I'd thought it was his legs bothering him. "I'm sorry, my love," I said. "I'm so sorry. I didn't know." Woodrow didn't respond.

"I recommend we take care of him here," the doctor said.

"No," I said. "I'm sorry to push back, but I won't agree to that. I promised him I would take him home."

"To be blunt, he could die before he gets there," she said. "I don't want to release him."

"Please," I said. "I have a home vet who can be there in an hour to help him. Please. Let me call her and have her talk to you."

"All right," said the doctor. "But this is against my judgment."

"Thank you," I said, and took the phone into the hallway. I called Dr. Mimi, even though it was 5:30 a.m. She didn't pick up, so I called again. I texted her the situation and paced the hall. She called me back.

"What's happening, lovemuffin?" she asked.

I told her. "I'm so sorry, sweetie," she said. "But I think you need to consider letting him go."

"I will," I said. "I promise. But not here. At home. On his bed, surrounded by his toys. That was my plan. This isn't in my plan."

As I said it, I knew how ridiculous it was. Death was not a respecter of plans. My parents had taught me that. But Dr. Mimi said, "Let me talk to the doctor."

I carried the phone back into the ER and handed it to the vet. She had a terse chat with Dr. Mimi while I petted and whispered reassurance to Woodrow. The vet gave me my phone.

"I told her I would make him comfortable," she said. "I'm going to give him more morphine. Then I will release him. You understand this is against my recommendation. She will come to your house in an hour. Otherwise I would not let him go."

"Yes," I said, "I understand."

"I'm going to get him ready," she said. "We'll bring him out to you."

"Thank you," I said.

I went out to the waiting room. The sun was coming up over the parking lot, fine and golden. I thought of the last lines from *Sophie's Choice*: "This was not judgment day—only morning. Morning: excellent and fair." I had an hour. I called Jacqulene. "Jenna?" she said on the first ring. "What is it?"

"I'm at the Angell," I said. Every dog owner knew what that meant. I started to cry. "Woodrow's going," I said. "I'm going to bring him home. Will you please help me carry him inside?"

"Of course," she said. She was crying, too. "It will be an honor."

I called Kate and asked her to come, too, left word for Sara. I texted Elizabeth Berg to say I was so sorry to contact her so early but there would be no dog and cake that day. I called Jim. "No!" he said. "No. Are you sure? His stomach?"

"I know," I said. "That's what I said."

"I just can't believe it," he said. "Can you wait? Can you wait until I get there?"

"I don't think so," I said. "The vet will only release him if Dr. Mimi comes right away. I'm so sorry."

"I'm leaving as soon as I can," he said.

"I have to go," I said. "He's coming out now."

The vet helped me lift Woodrow from the gurney into the Jeep: not the back seat, where he had spent so many hours riding, but the wayback, which she lined with blankets and towels. Woodrow's eyes were open a slit, but he was still unresponsive. "I've given him more morphine," the vet said. She stepped back. She was a small woman with dark hair, shorter than I was. "I'm sorry," she said.

"I'm sorry, too," I said. "That I asked you to go against your principles. But I really appreciate it. Thank you."

She touched me on the arm. "Good luck," she said.

I drove Woodrow home for the last time. The sun rose farther, above the trees; it was a beautiful morning, pink and gold. Around us, commuters sipped coffee in their cars. I talked to Woodrow about all the trips we had taken in this vehicle: "Remember when we drove back and forth to your Blue House in Minnesota?" I said. "And how we stopped in your favorite hotel in Ohio and I always said,

'What is this wonderful place?' And the staff came outside and said 'It's the *Woodrow!*' and gave you lots of treats? And how we drove to Montana with Jim, and Florida to see Pom Fran"—my mom—"and Brother? And we went to Kansas, and Texas, and to the woods and the beach, remember?" I tried not to cry. I didn't want him to hear me cry. I knew somewhere, wherever he was, he could hear me. "Today you are going on another trip," I said. "I can't go with you this time, Kooks. I'm sorry about that. But you will go to a beautiful place, and Pom Fran will be there, and my dad, who you never met, and they will take care of you, they will be so happy to see you. It is a good day to take a trip," I said, "a beautiful day to go."

When I pulled up in front of our building, Jacqulene was waiting for us, and so was Kirsten. I had asked Kirsten to be on hand to move my Jeep while Jacqulene and I took Woodrow inside, since parking was notoriously tight in our neighborhood. But there was not only one spot right in front of our door, there were two. I parked and opened the tailgate. Woodrow was breathing deeply, peacefully. "Hi, buddy," Jacqulene said. She wiped her eyes. Woodrow didn't move. "We're going to take you inside," she said.

As she reached in, Sarah and Harriet came down the sidewalk. "Hi, guys!" Sarah called, and then she saw our faces. "Oh no," she said.

"Do you want to come say goodbye?" I said.

"Of course," she said. She came to the Jeep and leaned in.

"Oh, Woodrow," she said. We were all crying except Harriet, who sat next to Sarah, unusually quiet. Woodrow's nostrils twitched. He was doing sniffs. He knew where he was, on his street, right across from his bench. "We love you so much, Woodrow," said Sarah, and then Jacqulene lifted him and carried him up our building's steps one last time.

She got him settled on his bed in my study, beneath the loft, and we sat around him and waited for Dr. Mimi, Kirsten near Woodrow's tail and I near his head, Jacqulene with her back against the wall. "Of course he's surrounded by beautiful ladies, as always," I said, and we all laughed. "See, Kooks?" I said. "You are home on your nice bed, just like I promised." Woodrow's eyes were closed. His breathing was even. Around him were all his friends: his avocado with its tennis-ball pit, his hot dog and carrots and musical birthday cake, his giant cow and Stinky Chickie.

Dr. Mimi arrived a few minutes later and sat on the floor with us. "Hi, lovemuffin," she said to Woodrow. She cradled his paw with its very old, smooth pads. "They left the port in," she said. "That's good." Taped to Woodrow's front leg was the tube where the IV had been, into which Dr. Mimi could put her own fatal medicine.

"Are you sure?" I said, looking at her. "Are you sure this is the right time?"

"Oh, sweetheart," she said. "He's in pain."

"But he seems fine," I said. I looked at Woodrow, sleeping so peacefully. "Can't we wait even until Jim gets here?"

I realized why the Angell vet had been so loath to let me take Woodrow home. "He doesn't seem like he's in pain," I said.

"That's because he's on morphine," said Dr. Mimi. "When it wears off, he'll be suffering. You could keep him with you another twenty-four hours, but you'd have to bring him back to Angell for more pain meds, and then you'd have to do it there."

I looked down at Woodrow, and some tears fell on his fur.

"Sweetie," said Dr. Mimi. "You asked me to tell you when it was time. It's time."

I looked at her somber freckled face, then at Kirsten, Kirsten who had known Woodrow when he was a puppy, had seen him run joyously through the woods with branches and jump into the waves. Tears ran down her face, but she nodded.

"He's had a wonderful life," she said.

I nodded. I looked at Jacqulene, who was also crying. She nodded, too.

"Okay," I said. "Okay."

I put my head down against Woodrow's, my forehead against his. I was aware of movement around me, the other women talking quietly to each other as Dr. Mimi made her preparations. I shut it all out. It was just me and Woodrow, his fur, his breathing. "Mommoo loves you, Kooks," I said. It was what I told him every night when I went to bed.

"I love you more than anybody in the universe. Yes, I do. Mommoo loves you more than anybody in the uni. Yes, she does. Mommoo loves you more than anybody else in the uni. Yes, she does. Mommoo loves you more than anybody else in the uni. Yes, she does."

It was so quiet. It was like with my mom: one minute Woodrow was breathing, and then he was not. I kept talking to him, repeating our catechism: *I love you more than anybody in the uni.* I listened for breaths. But there were no more. Finally I lifted my head. "Is he gone?" I asked.

Dr. Mimi laid her stethoscope against Woodrow's chest. "Yes, my love," she said. "He is."

"Is he really gone?" I asked. I looked at Kirsten and Jacqulene. They both nodded. I nodded, too. "Okay," I said. "But can he come back?"

I cried and cried, now that Woodrow was not here to hear me. "Oh, my dog," I said. "Oh, my good dog." I hugged him, his poor old beautiful body that had been through so much. I felt his fur on my forearms for the last time. I knew I would have to let him go, the physicality of him that I so loved, that had provided me with comfort and laughter and structure for all my days, and I would never see or feel it again. That would be the hardest part. Once his body was gone, it would be irrevocable.

Dr. Mimi was putting her kit away. "You did a good thing," she said. "He's lucky. He doesn't have to suffer. People don't have that luxury."

"I know," I said. "Thank you." She stood up. I stood up. Jacqulene lifted Woodrow, wrapped in a blanket, his head covered. She carried him down through the building and out to Dr. Mimi's car, which would take him to the funeral home. People stopped on the sidewalk to let us pass.

"Okay, Kooks," I said, when Jacqulene had slid Woodrow's body onto the back seat and stepped back. The blanket had fallen away and I could see his face. He did not look alive anymore; his upper lip had drawn back in a slight snarl. I didn't want to see him that way, so I covered him back up. I felt for the end of his tail, its thick wiry fur, and rubbed it between my fingertips. "I will see you again someday," I told him, "I love you," and then Dr. Mimi shut the door.

We stood on the sidewalk and watched her drive away, pulling into morning traffic as if it were any other day. "Well," I said, "he's gone," and then, as I had in the hospital, I bent over, there on the sidewalk, the force of my grief rendering me unable to stand. Kirsten and Jacqulene put their arms around me, encircling me, and we all cried together for a while. Then Kirsten said, finally, "Let's get you inside."

I wish I could say the rest of the day was a blur, but it wasn't. I did sleep, thanks to not having gotten any the night before. Or rather, I passed out on my couch. Kirsten canceled her meetings and sat across from me, keeping watch. I slept, dreamed of Woodrow—where was he?—and woke with a start. I felt deeply confused. My dog was gone, I knew this intellectually, but it made no sense. I felt the most profound dislocation. "Is it true?" I asked Kirsten. "He's gone?" She nodded. "Can he come back now?" I asked again. "I just want him back. I want my dog. I want my dog."

"I know," she said.

I drifted again. At some point Kate arrived. I went down to the lobby to let her in. She balked at the stairs. "I just don't know if I can stand to go in if he's not there," she said, and wept. We hugged. We went upstairs. She greeted Kirsten, and I heard them murmuring. I returned to the couch. The doorbell rang again and Kate went to answer it, coming back with flowers. "From your upstairs neighbors," she said. I looked at them. They were beautiful, white roses. "I don't want flowers," I said. "I want my dog."

"I know, honey," she said.

I slept and woke, slept and woke. I had an excruciating headache. More people kept coming, more flowers. Kate and Kirsten laundered Woodrow's bedding; I saw them walking in and out with piles of blankets in their arms. Sara came and sat with me, rubbed my back and did deep breathing, wrapped me in a blanket like a burrito. I was ungrateful. I did not want to be wrapped like a burrito. I kicked the blanket off. "I just want my dog," I said. Kate put food in my lap, a bowl of soup. "It's my bone broth," I heard Sara say. I just looked at it. I didn't know what to do with it. "Okay, let's take that away," Kate said, and the bowl was removed. I lay back down.

All that day I slept and woke. My dog was gone. Where was he? What if he needed me? "Do you think he's mad at me for not being there?" I asked Kate, who had replaced Kirsten. She was reading, drinking tea. She put her cup down. "He's never been without me," I said. "Do you think he's scared?"

"Oh, honey, no," she said. "He's still here. His body is gone, but he's still here with you."

But he wasn't. I dozed again, and when I woke it was dark. Kirsten was where Kate had been, the lamp turned on next to her. She handed me a glass of water. "Do you think you could eat anything? What sounds good?"

Nothing did, so she ordered comfort food: mac and cheese, mashed potatoes, creamed spinach, more soup. Soft food, convalescent. When it arrived, she set it out on plates on my dining room table and sat with me while I tried to eat. I took a couple of bites. "Thank you," I said. "Thank you for taking care of me." As we looked out at the Mall, toward Woodrow's bench, it suddenly lit up; thousands of white holiday lights glowed in the trees. I had forgotten tonight was Boston's tree-lighting ceremony. "They're shining for Woodrow this year," Kirsten said.

She stayed with me, rearranging her trip so I wouldn't

have to spend my first night without Woodrow alone. "Nighty night, Kooks," I said to his bed, the way I always did before going up to the loft. Contrary to what Kate had said, I didn't feel him there. I didn't feel him anywhere. It was the same way with my mom after she'd died: they were just gone. Somewhere else. "Mommoo loves you more than anybody in the universe," I said anyway. "Yes, she does."

In the morning I awoke to the little noises of somebody downstairs: Kate, making tea. "Good morning," she said. "Kirsten went to work. Would you like breakfast?"

All day people came and went, in shifts, handing the grief baton off to each other. They carried in the flowers that kept arriving. Casey brought over a photo of Woodrow, looking solemn by his bench, that she especially loved. Jenna P came over with BLTs and croissants and pastries and cried with me. Cat came in the evening and broke crackers and cheese into tiny pieces. "My grandmother Lynnie used to say when people are grieving, you should give them little bites," she explained. "It makes food easier for them to eat." She was right.

That second night Woodrow was gone, Jim arrived. He began crying the moment he saw me, in the vestibule. He grabbed me and embraced me so fiercely we both staggered. Everyone else withdrew, respectfully leaving us to our grief, our shared memories. *Remember Woodrow's Coolie Cave, that bush in the backyard he used to lie in when it was hot, thinking he was so sly, and then we'd say, "Where's Woodrow?"*

and the bush would wag? Remember how he used to chase us with the sprinkler? Remember how he could eat a whole DQ cone in one chomp? Remember how he was scared of flies—"Buzzies"? Remember how he used to help with the vacuuming and lawn mowing by dropping tennis balls in our path? Remember how he got carrots from the crisper drawer every time he came in from outside? How he carried five-pound bags of them in from the car? And the big SPLOOSHO when he dove into the water!

Cards kept coming, flowers, food. I posted the news of Woodrow's departure on social media, and the response was instant and overwhelming, literally thousands of messages pouring in. Elizabeth Berg wrote me a note: *Man, there never was a dog more loved.* Readers sent drawings and paintings of Woodrow from photos they had loved of him. Erin brought soup, my friend Tracy a challah. People sat with us, remembered with us. Every time a Woodrow memory hit me extra hard, I cried, and the crying hurt and gave me headaches, but I felt the memory itself was safely encapsulated, rising away from me in a balloon. It was what mourning was, the hard work of grief. Tracy said this was why Jews sat shiva, not only to help the mourner—who for a week wasn't permitted to leave her home—but so the community could help. And mine did. For years I had dreaded Woodrow's crossing, not only because I would lose him, his dear and particular self, but because I had feared I would be completely alone. Yet since he had gone, I had not been alone for a single minute. They had been with me all the time, my friends and neighbors, surrounding me, taking care of me. It was because of Woodrow, because they had loved him, too. And it was because of him that I had learned to let them in.

One afternoon three or four days in, there was a knock at the apartment door, and when I opened it, I found John the Shakespearian maintenance guy there. He was standing sideways, holding out a bag at arm's length, his head turned away. "I can't look at you," he said, "or I'll lose it. I just wanted you to have this."

"Thank you so much," I said, taking the bag. "Won't you come in?"

"No," he said. "Thank you. I'm sorry," and he went down the stairs.

Inside the bag was a beautiful white star orchid. "Wow, look what John the maintenance guy brought us," I said to Jim. I set the plant on the table and took the little card from its envelope. *For Woodrow, the newest little star in the heavens,* it read. *'Tis a fearful thing to love / what death can touch.*

Woodrow Memorials

Casey Cokkinias: photo & orchid

Caroline & Patrick Kelly: orchid

Jamie & Jamie: orchid

John the maintenance guy: orchid

Patrick the mailman: poem

Betsy Maxwell: holiday ornament with photo of Woodrow and me
on the road

Claudete Rizzotto, my stylist: black hair tinsel & rose

Dolce & the Yalcin family: note in bucket

Laura and Violet, dog family: card in bucket

Jenna Paone: card & BLTs

Bjorn Standhal, age nine: drawings

Dell & Liz Smith: card

Trisha Blanchet: card

Mo Haney & Finley, her beagle: card (& memorial)

Katie Hayes: card (& memorial)

Tracy Hahn-Burket: challah

Erin Almond: soup

South Bay: card & donation to Angell

Amy Haid: card

Christiane Alsop: card & gold-painted leaves

My Grub Street Master Novel class: card

Ericka & Ian Gray: donation to the Angell

Eileen Bagley & Spike: card

Allison & Atticus: card

Cathy Elcik: card

Lynda Loigman: silver frame

Sara DiVello: candle

Dr. Mimi Krieger: card & box

Whitney Scharer: card

Maddie Houpt: card

Casey's mom, Regina Cokkinias: card

June Banet: book, *Dog Heaven*

Epilogue

January

THE TREAT BUCKET

When Woodrow was about six, I went through a bad breakup, in the aftermath of which Woodrow looked at me with daily annoyance as I cried. *Pull it together, Mommoo. You are not tending to me the way you should.* I told my therapist that in the wake of the event, I didn't want to eat because it would be the first meal without my love. Or wash my face, because I'd be removing the makeup I'd worn when I'd last seen him. Or change my clothes, or watch TV, or shower—each thing done without him carrying me further and further away. My therapist nodded. "You're talking about grief," she said.

As the days wore on after Woodrow's death, each taking him further from us, we honored him as best we could. We held a memorial for him on the bench. It was a dozen beautiful ladies and Jim, just as Woodrow would have wanted it. Jim and I spoke; Sara read the Mary Elizabeth Frye poem "Do Not Stand by My Grave and Weep"; we lit candles; we played a recording from my friend Stacy, who sings gospel, singing "Amazing Grace." We left a framed photo of smiling young Woodrow on the bench, votives in a semicircle in front of it; it stayed intact for days, in the sleet and snow and sun. A local paper did a segment on it— "Friends Remember Woodrow, Who Was a Good Boy." Sometimes when I went out to the bench I found gifts. Like notes: *Dear Woodrow's Family, we always loved seeing you out here. We miss you!* Roses, wedged beneath the photo. Bones and rawhides, which were swiftly whisked away by the neighborhood dogs, and commemorative rocks and pebbles, which stayed.

One of the things Woodrow had loved to do most, right up until he went into heart failure, was go to the treat bucket. This was a small lidded can four blocks away on the Exeter-Fairfield block of Commonwealth, lashed to its own park bench with a bicycle lock and chain. The neighbors on that block kept it filled with treats: Milk-Bones; sweet potato and salmon bites; peanut butter puffs that looked like Cheetos. Even when he could barely walk, if Woodrow suddenly decided he wanted to go to the treat bucket, he made it there in record time, stumping along with great determination, trailing his harness behind him. Once he saw the bucket, his stiff gait quickened. He pushed the lid off with his snout like a bear—*clang!*, it went on the cement—and stuck his whole head in. "It's not a trough," I'd say, tugging his collar. "That's enough! We have to leave some for the other dogs." Woodrow had very little sense of civic responsibility: *I do not agree with this sharing thing, Mommoo.* Going back took us three times as long, as Woodrow always wanted to return to the bucket. *Are you crazy?* his face said, as I glided backward away from him, holding out treats in my hands to entice him. *You are leaving the treats! There are MORE treats in there!* Sometimes I'd cave and we'd go back to the bucket three, four times before I finally took him home.

About a week after Woodrow's death, a box arrived from Amazon. It was light and came up to my kneecaps. Inside was a white metal bucket with a line drawing of a Lab on it, and a bicycle chain and a lock. I already had the treats, Woodrow's supply of Milk-Bone Minis in the coat closet. I took everything out to the bench.

It was a chilly gray afternoon not long before Christmas. The snow that had fallen the last week of Woodrow's life, that he had lain in to cool his belly, had blown away except for a couple of dingy patches here and there. People hurried past in their parkas and gloves and hats, incurious about what I was doing, sparing a glance at most. I set the bucket next to the bench, in the depression of bare dirt where Woodrow used to lie, where he'd worn the grass away with his body. I threaded the bike lock chain through the bucket's handle and its lid, then secured the combination lock with the dates of Woodrow's birthday.

I put the Milk-Bones inside and pushed the lid back on, and to the front with clear packing tape I affixed a photo in a laminated sleeve of Woodrow lying next to the bench, wearing his harness and a huge happy smile. The caption said:

PLEASE ENJOY THESE TREATS COURTESY OF
WOODROW, WHO LOVED THIS BENCH!
09/30/04–12/05/19

I kissed my fingers and touched the photo of Woodrow. "Mommoo loves you, Kooks," I said. "More than anybody in the universe." It seemed there should be more to do, more to say. I hated to leave the bucket. I stood there in the cold wind for a few seconds more, understanding for the first time why people tend graves. Then I went inside.

"It's up," I said to Jim, who had been working.

"The treat bucket? It's on the bench?"

"It's on the bench," I said. "Come see."

We went to the bay window in the library and looked out. From where I was standing on Woodrow's sheepskin rug, we had a clear sightline to the bench and the bucket attached to it. It looked very small under the big trees.

A dog and owner came walking along, the woman hunched in her jacket, the dog trotting briskly. The dog noticed the bucket and tacked toward it. "Come on," Jim and I said under our breath.

The owner yanked the dog away. "Boo!" I said. "Grinch."

Another dog owner came from the opposite direction, tugged along by a pair of Pekingese. "Forget it," I said, "they're not really treat dogs." I was right. The trio passed the bucket.

"We should put a walkie-talkie in the bucket," Jim said. "Then whoever passes by without stopping, we can yell, 'Hey, dumbbell! Your dog needs treats!'"

"Good idea," I said.

A man with a little blond French bulldog came down the path. Dolce, I thought her name was. I didn't know them very well, but we'd had a couple of pleasant conversations on the bench. "Come on, you can do it," Jim said.

"I'm not optimistic," I said. "Frenchies aren't big treat whores either."

But Dolce spotted the bucket and tacked toward it. Her owner stopped and bent, I assumed to read the inscription on the Woodrow photo. Then, as Jim and I held our breath, he opened the lid, made Dolce sit, and took a treat out. Jim and I yelled in triumph as Dolce got the treat, chewing happily, and they walked on.

"They did it!" Jim said. We high-fived. "It works!"

"Woodrow's treat bucket is officially open for business!" I said. "Wait, I have an idea."

I got the string of bells from the front doorknob, where I'd hung it when Woodrow was a youngster for him to nudge with his snout whenever he needed to go outside.

It had been a while since he'd used it, but the bells made a cheerful noise whenever we came or went, so I'd left them there. I brought them to the window seat now.

"We should ring these whenever a dog gets a treat," I suggested. "And every time that happens, maybe an angel dog gets its wings. Or is that too corny?"

"Not at all," Jim said. "I think Woodrow would approve."

"Woodrow would push all the other dogs out of the way to get the treats, is what he would do," I said.

We sat on the window seat, surveying Woodrow's kingdom, lying in wait. Every time a dog owner came along, paused, and stopped, we urged him on. When the dog got a treat, or several, we cheered and rang the bells. I don't know whether an angel dog really got its wings or not when this happened. I don't know if there is any such thing. But I do think Woodrow would have liked this; he would have stuck his whole head in the bucket himself. *Mommoo, look, treats! It is the best day ever!* All afternoon and into the evening we watched as dogs came and went to the bucket on Woodrow's bench, the lights coming on in the big trees.

Do not stand at my grave and weep.
I am not there. I do not sleep.
I am a thousand winds that blow.
I am the diamond glints on snow.
I am the sunlight on ripened grain.
I am the gentle autumn rain.
When you awaken in the morning's hush
I am the swift uplifting rush
Of quiet birds in circled flight.
I am the soft stars that shine at night.
Do not stand at my grave and cry;
I am not there. I did not die.

—*Mary Elizabeth Frye*

Acknowledgments

It's my hope that this whole book serves as a love letter to the people in it who taught and helped me and Woodrow so much. But you can never say "thank you" too many times. So with all my heart, thank you to:

Erin Almond for the Frosty Paws.

Andrew Ballantine for finding Woodrow and Smarty.

Jacqulene Brzozowski for being Woodrow's honor guard.

Mark Cecil for changing this whole book by encouraging me to go deeper. You That Breau.

Casey Cokkinias, Alyson Pittman, and Caroline Ward, who cared for Woodrow so beautifully in his extremity.

Erin Connors for keeping Woodrow company in his poolie.

Elizabeth, Bram, and Miss Amelia DeVeer, for visiting us.

Sara DiVello and Allen Nunally for bone broth, dog-parent empathy, and sitting on the floor so often with me and my old boy.

Cathy Elcik for the chicken breasts.

Kym Havens for the banquet and lilies.

Julie Hirsch for being my one, my only Puppet.

Stephen Kiernan for bacon and limericks.

Kirsten Liston for being Boss Lady, Answer Girl, and there at the right time. I think you did that rather well.

Cat Mazur for shining light and tiny bites.

Jenna Paone for writing days, crying with me, and the BLT.

Jane Roper for the divine spark beta read.

Kate Woodworth for Westport—the best days ever.

Special thanks to Judy Stoltzfus, wife of Jonas Stoltzfus for fifty-six years. While I was working on this memoir, Jonah passed away. Judy was unfailingly generous in providing me with Jonah's poetry even in the midst of her grief. I am so glad Woodrow and I met them.

The dog moms and dads of Commonwealth Avenue: Eileen Bagley, Allison Hirsch, Deb Knez; Jamie Kotch and Jamie Corkindale; Mike McCart; Monique Momjian and family; Mary Norling-Christensen, Sarah Whitlock: thank you for your good company. And the doormen at the Taj Hotel, Boston; our talented maintenance guy John Davin, and our mailmen Jeff Mossman and Patrick Lewis!

Woodrow's vets, who gave him such good care, love, and Easy Cheese: Drs. Baker, Bower, Gardiner, and Wosko and staff at South Bay Veterinary Clinic, Boston, Massachusetts; Dr. Jill Kindermann and staff at LaCrosse Veterinary Clinic, LaCrosse, Wisconsin; Dr. Michelle "Mimi" Krieger; Dr. Christen Skaer and her staff at Skaer Vet, Wichita, Kansas; Dr. Wolf and staff at the Blue Pearl Pet Hospital, Eden Prairie, Minnesota; Dr. Joseph Zarin and the wonderful staff of MSPCA Angell, Boston, Massachusetts.

To all my friends who followed Woodrow on social media, thank you for keeping his memory and spirit alive! To name a handful: Elizabeth Berg; Kathy Crowley; Elizabeth, Bram, and Miss Amelia DeVeer; Tracy Hahn-Burket; Mo Hanley; Katie Hayes; Pam Jenoff; Lynda Loigman; Michelle Marie Martin, Betsy Blumberg Maxwell; Sarah McCoy; Alyson Richman; Claudete Rizzotto; Stacy Williams . . . I need a whole second book to recognize everyone! I see you and love you all.

Robin Kall Homonoff, Pamela Klinger-Horn, Susan McBeth, Andrea Peskind-Katz, Margy Stratton: the tireless good angels of literature. Thank you for everything you do, seen and unseen, every day.

Bookstore owners and staff, librarians, hosts, and readers at all my events, from San Diego to South Beach, Minnesota to Maine, Dallas to the Dakotas, the littlest book club to the biggest auditorium: bless you all. I can't wait to see you again—I don't care where or how, just bring it! THANK YOU for reading. Special holla to the Jewish Book Council for giving me my Maisel mic and welcoming me into your communities.

My novelists at Grub Street Writers, my literary home for more than twenty years—you know who you are, you scary crew, you glitterati. Trisha Blanchet, Hillary Casavant, Mark Cecil, Tom Champoux, Chuck Garabedian, Julie Gerstenblatt, Kimberly Hensle Lowrance, Edwin Hill, Alex Hoopes, Sonya Larson, Kirsten Liston, Joe Moldover, Jenna Paone, Jane Roper, Whitney Scharer,

Adam Stumacher, Grace Talusan, Kate Woodworth, I love you to the last page and beyond. Even with puppets.

My Mighty Blaze fam: thank you for the joy you bring me—and countless writers and readers!—every day. Caroline Leavitt, especially looking at you for being my first reader and making me ugly cry with your kindness. My fierce Blaze and *Woodrow* publicist, Laura "GlenGarry Glen BossiRossi"—love you more.

My wonderful editor, Sara Nelson, whom I adore as much as I respect. You have given me and my books the warmest home. Thank you for your belief in me! My beloved publicist, Katherine Beitner: Kol Hakavod. Miranda Ottewell for brilliantly and conscientiously copyediting another book. Mary Gaule for crying over Woodrow, gentle proofreading, and patience with my stubborn Adobe Acrobat ineptitude. Joanne O'Neill for putting my old boy on this beautiful cover and Bonni Leon-Berman for the gorgeous interior design. The HarperCollins team who magically transposed this manuscript into a book: thank you.

My incomparable agent, Stéphanie Abou, my right arm. *Je t'aime, Madame.* Here's to many more decades of coproducing books and world domination.

My family: Joey Blum and Kristin Barton; Lesley M.M. Blume-Macek, Greg Macek, Oona Helene-Macek; my Joerg cousins and my uncle Lowell; my aunt Judy Blum. My mom Franny and dad Bob, who I hope are feeding Woodrow bacon across that big river. You guys are my guiding constellation always.

Jim Reed for being the world's best dog dad. Carrots, car rides, countless photos, and videos . . . There are not enough words to adequately express all the love, laughter and joy. I know Woodrow's memory lives most strongly in you.

To every friend and stranger who stopped by Woodrow's bench: thank you.

About the Author

JENNA BLUM is the *New York Times* and number one internationally bestselling author of novels *Those Who Save Us*, *The Stormchasers*, and *The Lost Family*. She was voted one of Oprah readers' Top 30 Women Writers on Oprah.com and is the cofounder and CEO of the literary social media marketing company A Mighty Blaze. Jenna earned her MA at Boston University in creative writing and has taught writing workshops at Grub Street Writers for more than twenty years. She interviewed Holocaust survivors for Steven Spielberg's Survivors of the Shoah Visual History Foundation and is a professional public speaker, traveling nationally and internationally to speak about her work. Jenna is based in downtown Boston, where she lives across from Woodrow's bench and is currently a dog mom to her black Lab puppy Henry Higgins. For more about Jenna, please visit www.jennablum.com and follow her on Facebook, Twitter, and Instagram.